1st EDITION

The Vietnam War

1st EDITION

The Vietnam War

David Haugen and Susan Musser

Book Editors

GREENHAVEN PRESS
A part of Gale, Cengage Learning

Detroit • New York • San Francisco • New Haven, Conn • Waterville, Maine • London

Christine Nasso, *Publisher*
Elizabeth Des Chenes, *Managing Editor*

For more information, contact:
Greenhaven Press
27500 Drake Rd.
Farmington Hills, MI 48331-3535
Or you can visit our Internet site at gale.cengage.com.

For product information and technology assistance, contact us at
Gale Customer Support, 1-800-877-4253.

For permission to use material from this text or product, submit all requests online at
www.cengage.com/permissions.

Further permissions questions can be e-mailed to permissionrequest@cengage.com.

Articles in Greenhaven Press anthologies are often edited for length to meet page requirements. In addition, original titles of these works are changed to clearly present the main thesis and to explicitly indicate the author's opinion. Every effort is made to ensure that Greenhaven Press accurately reflects the original intent of the authors. Every effort has been made to trace the owners of copyrighted material.

Cover image Custom Medical Stock Photo, Inc. Reproduced by permission.

LIBRARY OF CONGRESS CATALOGING-IN-PUBLICATION DATA

The Vietnam War / David Haugen and Susan Musser, book editors.
    p. cm. -- (Perspectives on modern world history)
    Includes bibliographical references and index.
ISBN 978-0-7377-5008-9 (hardcover)
1. Vietnam War, 1961–1975--Sources--Juvenile literature. 2. Vietnam War, 1961–1975--United States--Sources--Juvenile literature. I. Haugen, David M., 1969- II. Musser, Susan.
    DS557.4.V568 2011
    959.704'3--dc22   2010039241

Printed in the United States of America
1 2 3 4 5 6 7 15 14 13 12 11

CONTENTS

most popular magazines claims that the lack of progress in pacifying Vietnam, the steadfastness of the Communist enemy, and the mounting U.S. casualties have turned Americans and their representatives against the war.

CHAPTER 2   Controversies Surrounding the Vietnam War

America's priority is to make good on its promise to defend freedom at home and abroad. By securing democracy for foreign lands beset by tyrants and Communists, the president foresees a new world order in which all nations will work cooperatively toward peace.

unjustly involved in what is essentially a civil
war and is destroying villages and their inhabitants in a perverse attempt to stop the reunification of a sovereign land.

Vietnamese army describes how he had no desire to join the military until a U.S. bomb killed his fiancée. He joins the army to avenge her death despite protests from his family.

FOREWORD

*"History cannot give us a program for the future,
but it can give us a fuller understanding of ourselves, and of our common humanity, so that we
can better face the future."*

—Robert Penn Warren,
American poet and novelist

The history of each nation is punctuated by mo-
mentous events that represent turning points for
that nation, with an impact felt far beyond its borders. These events—displaying the full range of human
capabilities, from violence, greed, and ignorance to heroism, courage, and strength—are nearly always complicated and multifaceted. Any student of history faces the
challenge of grasping the many strands that constitute
such world-changing events as wars, social movements,
and environmental disasters. But understanding these
significant historic events can be enhanced by exposure
to a variety of perspectives, whether of people involved
intimately or of ones observing from a distance of miles
or years. Understanding can also be increased by learning about the controversies surrounding such events and
exploring hot-button issues from multiple angles. Finally,
true understanding of important historic events involves
knowledge of the events' human impact—of the ways
such events affected people in their everyday lives—all
over the world.

Perspectives on Modern World History examines
global historic events from the twentieth-century on-
ward by presenting analysis and observation from numerous vantage points. Each volume offers high school,
early college level, and general interest readers a the-

matically arranged anthology of previously published materials that address a major historical event, with an emphasis on international coverage. Each volume opens with background information on the event, then presents the controversies surrounding that event, and concludes with first-person narratives from people who lived through the event or were affected by it. By providing primary sources from the time of the event, as well as relevant commentary surrounding the event, this series can be used to inform debate, help develop critical thinking skills, increase global awareness, and enhance an understanding of international perspectives on history.

Material in each volume is selected from a diverse range of sources, including journals, magazines, newspapers, nonfiction books, personal narratives, speeches, congressional testimony, government documents, pamphlets, organization newsletters, and position papers. Articles taken from these sources are carefully edited and introduced to provide context and background. Each volume of Perspectives on Modern World History includes an array of views on events of global significance. Much of the material comes from international sources and from U.S. sources that provide extensive international coverage.

Each volume in the Perspectives on Modern World History series also includes:

- A full-color **world map**, offering context and geographic perspective.
- An annotated **table of contents** that provides a brief summary of each essay in the volume.
- An **introduction** specific to the volume topic.
- For each viewpoint, a brief **introduction** that has notes about the author and source of the viewpoint, and that provides a summary of its main points.
- Full-color **charts**, **graphs**, **maps**, and other visual representations.

- Informational **sidebars** that explore the lives of key individuals, give background on historical events, or explain scientific or technical concepts.
- A **glossary** that defines key terms, as needed.
- A **chronology** of important dates preceding, during, and immediately following the event.
- A **bibliography** of additional books, periodicals, and Web sites for further research.
- A comprehensive **subject index** that offers access to people, places, and events cited in the text.

Perspectives on Modern World History is designed for a broad spectrum of readers who want to learn more about not only history but also current events, political science, government, international relations, and sociology—students doing research for class assignments or debates, teachers and faculty seeking to supplement course materials, and others wanting to improve their understanding of history. Each volume of Perspectives on Modern World History is designed to illuminate a complicated event, to spark debate, and to show the human perspective behind the world's most significant happenings of recent decades.

INTRODUCTION

From 1946 to 1954, France fought the First Indochina War to hold onto its colony in Vietnam. For the French government and its military, the struggle was too much to bear; the Viet Minh—the independence army that had aided the Allies in battling Japanese forces that held the region in World War II—were determined and resilient enough to throw off the yoke of colonial control. When the war ended, Ho Chi Minh, one of the Communist leaders of the Viet Minh, became its figure-head. Ho agreed to a partition of the country along the seventeenth parallel with the assurance that nationwide elections would quickly ensue, presumably uniting the nation under socialist rule. While Ho and the Viet Minh armies retreated to North Vietnam to await the promised elections, a new nationalist government was established in the South under Emperor Bao Dai, the heir to the dynastic throne that ruled Vietnam when the French were in power. Bao Dai lived in France during his brief one-year stint as the head of the newly formed State of Vietnam; he was summarily ousted by his chosen prime minister, Ngo Dinh Diem, in 1955. Diem founded the Republic of South Vietnam and ostensibly replaced the empire with a democratic state. Diem refused to be a partner in national elections that quite probably would have rejoined North and South Vietnam. Impressed with the hundreds of thousands of Christian refugees from the North that fled south to the Republic to escape religious persecution, Diem believed he could maintain control of South Vietnam and resist any attempts by the Communist North to reunify the nation. One of Diem's advisors was CIA attaché Colonel Edward Lansdale, who urged the prime minister to secure power in the South. It was at this point that the United States first became enmeshed in the power struggle between North and South Vietnam that would lead to another war in Southeast Asia.

Although the presidential administration of Dwight Eisenhower initially encouraged Diem to respect the accords that required national elections, several factors influenced U.S. politicians to rethink their advice and support the republic. First of all, Diem had toured the United States in the early 1950s, making influential friends with legislators and powerbrokers who were virulently anti-Communist. One such ally was John F. Kennedy, then an outspoken senator from Massachusetts who shared Diem's religious affiliation (Catholic) and his opinions that communism should be thwarted from gaining any more ground in Asia. Kennedy was fearful that a "Red Tide" would wash across Burma, Laos, and other Southeast Asian countries if freedom-lovers chose not to take up arms on behalf of South Vietnam if it were invaded by the North. In a 1956 speech at the Vietnam Conference in Washington, D.C., Kennedy also recognized that "the independence of a Free Vietnam is crucial to the free world in fields other than the military. Her economy is essential to the economy of Southeast Asia; and her political liberty is an inspiration to those seeking to obtain or maintain their liberty in all parts of Asia."

In addition to fearing the spread of communism, politicians understood the prestige and value of standing up to the threat. Two years prior to the founding of Diem's republic, the United States and its allies had concluded a successful war against Chinese forces and North Korean Communists on the Korean peninsula. Although the cost was high, the United States had proved itself willing to face the Communist tide and, as a result, had earned the respect of world leaders who favored the preservation of democracies—even if the protected or salvaged nations were democratic in name only. This national prestige dovetailed with the last factor that influenced

American officials to back Diem's regime: The United States had to answer the call of any imperiled democracy.

Though President Eisenhower was reluctant to commit U.S. troops to Southeast Asia so soon after the Korean War, he understood that idleness would leave South Vietnam vulnerable to Communist subversion. Polls showed that despite the strong concentration of Christians in the republic, Ho Chi Minh was as popular a leader in the South as he was in the North. To counter the Communist influence, Eisenhower sent U.S. advisors to train Diem's fledgling nationalist army for possible war with the North, and he permitted the CIA to frustrate Communist insurrection and quash political rivals and dissent in the South. The Eisenhower administration also allocated funding and arms to Diem's cause, beginning the United States' active defense of South Vietnam.

Between 1955 and 1965, the American public was overwhelmingly in support of government policies toward Vietnam. Occasionally, events transpired that made Americans question whether the South Vietnamese government was as committed to democracy as it proclaimed, but U.S. policy was generally never in doubt. For example, when John F. Kennedy assumed the presidency in 1960, the Diem regime had been losing popularity both at home and abroad for some time. Diem's roundups of political enemies, his failed land redistribution policies, and his conflicts with the large Buddhist population of South Vietnam cast him as a tyrant. Americans showed concern over Diem's actions, but still held that South Vietnam was worth defending. Eventually, a South Vietnamese military plot—with U.S. collusion—orchestrated the removal and execution of Diem in 1963 and paved the way for a series of puppet leaders that the U.S. government tried to portray to the public as more sympathetic to the democratic idealism that Diem failed to embrace. For the most part, the fall of Diem resolved reservations of most Americans, and the print and television reporters who covered the succession of new South Vietnamese leaders tended to portray them as earnest anti-Communists who appreciated U.S. aid. An editorial in the February 7, 1964, issue of *Time* described General Nguyen Khanh, who took over the reins of government in 1964, as able and tenacious, reporting that "U.S. military advisers consider him one of South Viet Nam's ablest corps commanders, one of the few in fact who would rather fight than sleep at night." Still, such tempered remarks commonly accompanied pointed assessments of South Vietnam's instability and lack of collective defiance of the North.

In March 1965, President Lyndon Johnson (who took office when President Kennedy was assassinated in November 1963) committed the United States to a ground war in Vietnam. With pro-Communist Viet Cong guerrilla forces waging successful attacks in the South, Johnson ordered 50,000 combat troops to stabilize the region and bolster the South Vietnamese defense. In a speech given at Johns Hopkins University the following month, Johnson explained why he chose this risky path: "We fight because we must fight if we are to live in a world where every country can shape its own destiny. . . . And only in such a world will our own freedom be finally secure." Drawing on the legacy he inherited, Johnson stated, "We are there because we have a promise to keep. Since 1954 every American President has offered support to the people of South Viet-Nam. . . . To dishonor that pledge, to abandon this small and brave nation to its enemies, and to the terror that must follow, would be an unforgivable wrong."

Reaction to President Johnson's controversial move was mixed. That same month, the Students for a Democratic Society—a university-based movement that had been around for five years protesting nuclear escalation and domestic policy—organized a march on the Oakland Army terminal in California, a point of departure for

U.S. troops heading for Vietnam. In April, they amassed roughly 20,000 protestors outside the U.S. Capitol in demonstration against pursuing the war. Although these protests made headlines, newspaper, magazine, and television reporters covered military action in Vietnam in the same way they had covered previous wars—by focusing on soldiers' stories that reflected the day-to-day heroism and even their beneficence toward the Vietnamese. In an Internet article titled "Television Coverage of the Vietnam War and the Vietnam Veteran," writer Erin McLaughlin claimed television reporters were especially eager to find heroes and show America's good deeds. "This coverage was generally very supportive of U.S. involvement in the war and of the soldier himself until 1967," McLaughlin asserts.

The antiwar movement, however, attracted more and more recruits as the number of military personnel sent to Vietnam increased while, at the same time, the death toll of American soldiers rose month after month. In 1967, just over 485,000 U.S. troops were deployed in Vietnam, and more than 11,000 U.S. service personnel died there—nearly twice as many victims as the previous year. While General William Westmoreland, the U.S. military commander in Vietnam, was predicting victory by the end of the year, the public and even President Johnson were skeptical. Dr. Martin Luther King, Jr., the newsworthy civil rights leader, spoke out against the United States' involvement in Vietnam from a moral perspective. With such luminaries joining the antiwar camp, the administration knew its adversaries posed a powerful, if not always united, front. Johnson sent Ho Chi Minh a personal letter in February pledging to end hostilities if the North would cease its infiltration of the South. Ho wrote back, claiming the United States was the aggressor and needed to cease its actions before peace could be discussed. He also contended that America was guilty of war crimes:

In South Viet-Nam a half-million American soldiers and soldiers from the satellite countries have resorted to the most inhumane arms and the most barbarous methods of warfare, such as napalm, chemicals, and poison gases in order to massacre our fellow countrymen, destroy the crops, and wipe out the villages. In North Viet-Nam thousands of American planes have rained down hundreds of thousands of tons of bombs, destroying cities, villages, mills, roads, bridges, dikes, dams and even churches, pagodas, hospitals, and schools.

Ho expected that the U.S. government would be held accountable for these atrocities, and in some respects it was. As the war dragged on, news reports began exposing U.S. soldiers at the brink of exhaustion and mental collapse. Some spoke openly of their fears and even hinted at resentment against the government for their predicament. Images of burning villages and the general chaos of fighting a guerrilla war—sometimes against the population the U.S. soldiers were supposed to be saving—brought the confusion and savagery of war to the American public. Despite the growing concern about America's moral certainty and about the progress of the war, a Gallup poll showed that 52 percent of Americans surveyed claimed that the United States had not made a mistake sending troops to Vietnam.

The turning point in public opinion occurred sometime between May and July of 1967. By then, Secretary of State Robert McNamara had admitted to a congressional committee that the bombing campaign against North Vietnam would not be effective enough to force a peace, suggesting that the North Vietnamese and Viet Cong had not been sufficiently weakened to bring them to the bargaining table. In addition, news sources leaked information that only one in ten U.S. military personnel in Vietnam were actively seeking out the enemy; the rest were tied down defending strategic regions or otherwise engaged in non-offensive operations. By the end of July, less than half of Americans polled believed it had not been a mistake to send troops to Vietnam. The percentage fell into the low forties in early 1968, when the Viet Cong and elements of the North Vietnamese army launched a coordinated offensive around the Tet holidays. Striking nearly every major city in the South, the Tet Offensive proved the North Vietnamese and their allies in the South were far from defeated. Although U.S. forces quickly quashed the attacks and inflicted crippling casualties on the enemy, the U.S. public ignored the statistics and focused on the images of the besieged U.S. embassy in Saigon and listened as trusted CBS news anchor Walter Cronkite hypothesized, "We are mired in a stalemate that could only be ended by negotiation, not victory." In the aftermath of Tet, President Johnson's approval rating dropped to 36 percent. The battle-worn chief executive told the American public that he would not seek reelection in the coming term.

In 1969, Johnson's successor, Richard Nixon, inherited a war that most Americans now disdained. The latest Gallup poll revealed that 49 percent of the public believed the war would drag on for at least another two years. In a televised speech in November 1969, Nixon told the nation that a "silent majority" of Americans believed the country's moral mission in Vietnam was not in doubt and explained his new plan to pull U.S. troops out of Vietnam slowly, turning the bulk of the fighting over to the South Vietnamese. The speech was a clever tactic to convince the nation that the government's war policy enjoyed more support than it did while still initiating the United States' withdrawal from Vietnam. Even though opposition to the war was growing—drawing in the youth movement, civil rights activists, media personalities, and politicians—one poll showed that 40 percent of Americans believed that the United States should leave its troops in Vietnam for as long as it took for "Vietnamization" to work. The following year, however, Nixon's policies played to both ends of the political spectrum, the war "hawks" and the peace "doves." He announced that the United States would withdraw 150,000 soldiers from Vietnam over the next year, but he then revealed his plans to launch a coordinated campaign that would send South Vietnamese and U.S. troops into neighboring Cambodia, a neutral country, to wipe out bases that the North Vietnamese were using to arm infiltrators in the South. The decision to invade Cambodia polarized Americans and led to violence. The antiwar movement staged demonstrations in many cities and garnered nationwide attention when students opposed to the Cambodian operation were fired on by National Guardsmen at Kent State University. At the same time, construction workers in several U.S. cities held rallies in support of Nixon's policies. In one particular incident in New York City, these blue-collar men attacked war protestors with hammers, fists, and boots. The war had come home to America.

In 1971, the trial of American soldiers who massacred Vietnamese civilians in the village of My Lai during a search and destroy operation in 1968 fueled the peace movement. The "doves" also gained a much needed endorsement by Vietnam Veterans Against the War, an organization of soldiers who had returned to the states disenchanted with their role in an unpopular war. These veterans staged a highly publicized protest in April 1971, when several members threw their war medals and other mementos over the fence that surrounds the Capitol building in Washington, D.C. Despite such visible opposition, Nixon's economic policy and his arms-limitation talks with the Soviet Union carried him into a second term as president. The fact that troop withdrawals over the years left only 27,400 service personnel in Vietnam at the beginning of 1972 also helped his reelection. Using National Security Advisor Henry Kissinger as a peace-broker, Nixon eventually obtained a deal with the North Vietnamese that would permit the U.S. to withdraw the remainder of its forces unmolested. In a national address in January 1973, Nixon told the American people that the war was at an end. "Your steadfastness in supporting our insistence on peace with honor has made peace with honor possible," Nixon informed his radio and television audiences. It would take two more years before all U.S. personnel were out of Vietnam, and in April 1975, South Vietnam fell to the Communist armies. America's unpopular war was over, but the stigma of defeat would follow the United States into subsequent decades, influencing President Ronald Reagan's uncompromising, anti-Soviet Cold War policy and President George W. Bush's decision to invade Iraq and Afghanistan. Its enduring image has remained disunified and provocative, invoking notions of loyalty, bravery, and commitment as well as destruction, failure, and betrayal. And within this image, pride and humiliation are joined so tightly yet so illogically that Americans recoil at the thought of any subsequent conflict turning into "another Vietnam."

World Map

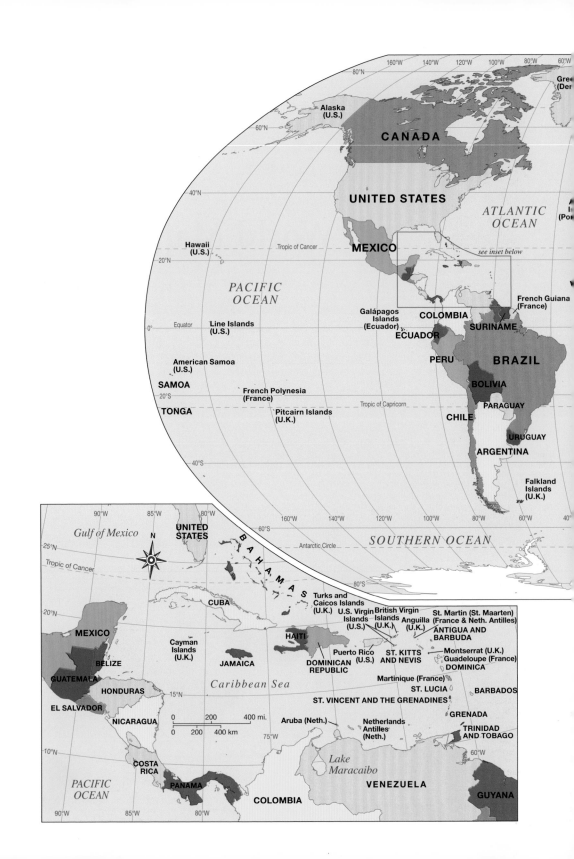

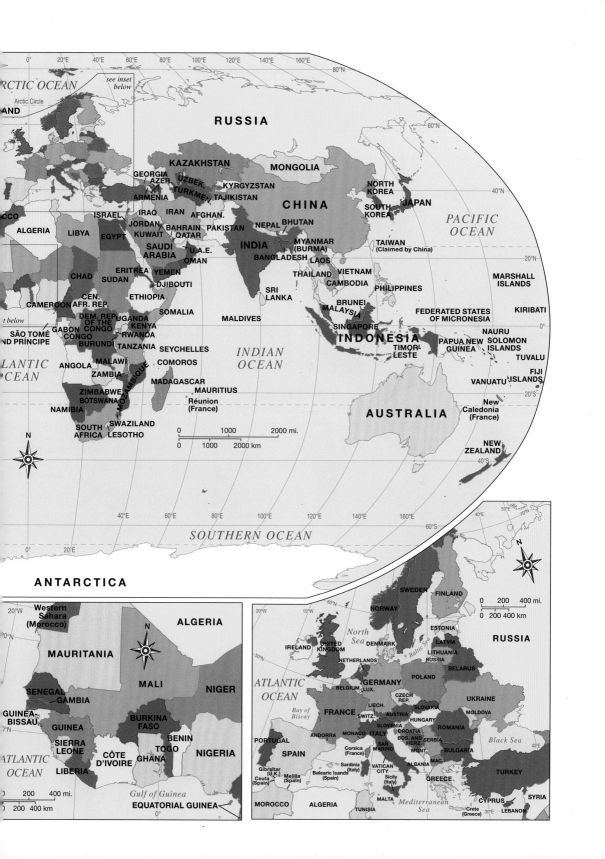

CHAPTER 1

Historical Background on the Vietnam War

The Vietnam War: An Overview

Gale Encyclopedia of U.S. Economic History

Following its liberation from French colonial status, Vietnam became a divided land plagued by civil war. Communist forces under Ho Chi Minh occupied the North, while a U.S.-backed regime declared a democracy in the South. Fearing that the Communists would engulf the entire region, U.S. presidents Dwight Eisenhower and John F. Kennedy offered economic and military aid to South Vietnam and committed the first U.S. soldiers (in an advisory capacity) to the region. The following viewpoint taken from the *Gale Encyclopedia of U.S. Economic History* describes how North Vietnamese incursions into the South eventually prompted the U.S. government to take more aggressive action to thwart the fall of South Vietnam. The United States became entangled in an all-out war in Vietnam during the presidency of Lyndon Johnson, eventually committing ground and air forces to buttress the democratic state. The war lasted from 1964 to 1975 and proved disastrous to the presidencies of Lyndon Johnson and his successor, Richard Nixon. As the number of U.S. casualties grew, the American home front

Photo on previous page: A fireball erupts as Vietcong rockets strike U.S. targets in South Vietnam. By its end, the Vietnam War was the longest war in U.S. history. (AP Images/Anonymous.)

SOURCE. Thomas Carson and Mary Bonk, *Gale Encyclopedia of U.S. Economic History*. © 2000 Gale, a part of Cengage Learning, Inc. Reproduced by permission. www.cengage.com.

turned against the war, ultimately influencing the U.S. govern-ment's decision to pull its troops out of the country and allow the South Vietnamese regime to fall to Communist forces.

The Vietnam War (1964–1975) was an eleven-year conflict in Southeast Asia between the American-backed government of South Vietnam and the Communist government of North Vietnam. The North Vietnamese sought to reunify the country following its partition in 1954, while the United States sought to contain Communist expansion by providing South Viet-nam with economic and military aid. U.S. involvement reached its peak in 1968–1969, when over five hundred thousand U.S. troops were on the ground. The Pentagon spent $77.8 billion to finance the war. Approximately 58,000 U.S. citizens and over three million Vietnam-ese were killed during the conflict. Two years after the United States withdrew in 1973, North Vietnamese forces defeated the South Vietnamese and reunified the country.

The French Lose Control of Vietnam

Vietnam entered the twentieth century as a French colony. During World War II (1939–1945) the French evacuated the colony and the Japanese occupied it. An indigenous nationalist resistance movement to the Japa-nese invaders sprang up under the leadership of Ho Chi Minh (1892–1969). Ho Chi Minh was a member of both the Vietnamese and the French Communist Parties and the preeminent leader of national self-determination in Vietnam. When the Japanese were defeated in 1945, the French returned to Vietnam and tried to reestablish their colonial authority. For 56 days, the nationalist Vietnam-ese military force (called the *Viet Minh*) besieged the French fort at Dien Bien Phu where several thousand

French troops were trapped. The French surrender led to peace talks in Geneva, Switzerland, in 1954. The treaty required withdrawal of all French troops from Vietnam and a temporary partition of the country at the 17th parallel, with Communists retreating to the north and non-Communists moving to the south. National elections to unify Vietnam were scheduled for 1956.

> " President Eisenhower harbored reservations about getting U.S. troops mired in another Asian conflict so soon after the Korean War. "

U.S. President Dwight D. Eisenhower (1953–1961) feared that in a national election Ho Chi Minh would defeat the American-supported president of South Vietnam, Ngo Dinh Diem (1955–1963). As a result, elections were held only in South Vietnam. But the elections were rigged and Diem won an overwhelming majority of the vote, declared his country's independence from North Vietnam, and named Saigon as its capital. The decision whether to support Diem was a difficult one for U.S. policymakers. On one hand the United States was concerned that without U.S. support, the South Vietnam government would collapse and fall to the Communists. On the other hand President Eisenhower harbored reservations about getting U.S. troops mired in another Asian conflict so soon after the Korean War (1950–1953).

Diem's Demise and the Rise of the Viet Cong

Diem's actions in office raised further concerns. His anti-Communist sympathies manifested themselves in harsh policies that alienated peasants and villagers. Diem, a Catholic, discriminated against Buddhists even though the Catholics made up only a small minority of the population that had played subordinate roles during the period of French colonialism. Opposition to Diem became widespread and in 1963 he was assassinated by elements in the Army. Diem's death was followed by ten successive South Vietnamese governments in 18 months.

Taking advantage of this upheaval, the nationalist guerilla forces in South Vietnam (called the People's Liberation Armed Forces (PLAF) or, colloquially, the "Viet Cong") emerged under the political leadership of the National Liberation Front. The NLF was an organization of broad nationalist forces, led by the Communist Party of Vietnam. Their goal was the reunification of North and South Vietnam.

The United States responded to these developments by increasing the number of U.S. military, economic, and political advisers in Vietnam from 800 in 1961, when President John F. Kennedy took office, to 16,700 in 1963. During the 1964 presidential race, Republican candidate Barry Goldwater charged President Lyndon B. Johnson (1963–1969), who took office following Kennedy's assassination, with not doing enough to win the war. Goldwater stated that Johnson would be responsible if Vietnam and its neighboring countries toppled like dominoes into the lap of the Communists.

The Tonkin Gulf Incident Pulls America Into War

Despite Goldwater's defeat, President Johnson was determined to not allow the so-called "domino theory" to become a reality. In August, 1964, U.S. ships off the coast of North Vietnam, in the Gulf of Tonkin, reported sonar indications of a torpedo attack. In response, Johnson ordered an air attack on North-Vietnamese ship bases and oil facilities. The next day the Senate granted the president's request for broad powers over the Southeast Asian conflict by passing the Gulf of Tonkin Resolution. The resolution gave the president authority to take

> By the end of [1965] the initial commitment of 3,500 [U.S.] troops [in Vietnam] had increased to 80,000.

Secretary of Defense Robert McNamara describes the alleged attack by North Vietnam on the United States in the Gulf of Tonkin on August 4, 1964. The attack was later brought into question. (AP Images/ Bob Schutz.)

all measures necessary to repel any further armed aggression against U.S. forces in the area.

Johnson relied on this "blank check" to commit the first U.S. combat troops to Vietnam on March 8, 1965. By the end of the year the initial commitment of 3,500 troops had increased to 80,000. These combat troops fought alongside the South Vietnamese armed forces, known as the Army of the Republic of Vietnam (ARVN). The ARVN was a poorly led group that lacked cohesion and motivation. In 1965 alone 113,000 ARVN troops were lost to desertion. Many U.S. soldiers disliked and mistrusted the ARVN and accused them of cowardice.

America's Home Front Turns Against the War

As the war dragged on in Vietnam, the anti-war movement picked up at home. Promises of victory by politicians and military commanders wore thin on an U.S. public confronted nightly by television images of bloody battles that accompanied mounting casualties. The credibility of U.S. government reports predicting imminent U.S. victory was further eroded by the 1968 Tet Offensive, an all-out assault on every major city in South Vietnam. The NLF forces suffered staggering losses during their offensive and made few strategic gains. The Viet Cong were virtually wiped out. But, though Tet was a military catastrophe for the NLF, it was a political victory. It took both U.S. and ARVN forces by surprise and had a resounding effect on the U.S. public.

> In 1969 opinion polls showed that for the first time in the war, a majority of respondents were opposed to the war.

The war had reached a stalemate and the Tet Offensive forced U.S. citizens to confront how deeply Communist resistance was entrenched throughout Vietnam. In 1969 opinion polls showed that for the first time in the war, a majority of respondents were opposed to the war. But, even though the war was becoming unpopular, most people were reluctant to pull out of Vietnam immediately. For a time, the American people were still willing to stand by the President in the struggle against Communism. Only between 20 and 40 percent of U.S. citizens polled in 1969 favored immediate withdrawal. But the protests were becoming larger and more frequent. And one by one, mainstream organizations and politicians began demanding peace in Vietnam. Inflation and higher taxes resulting from the war soured still other segments of society. It was no surprise that upon taking the oath of office in January, 1969, President Richard

Nixon (1969–1974) promised to end the war with honor. But before he ended the war, President Nixon and his Secretary of State, Henry Kissinger, widened it.

A Slow U.S. Withdrawal

In March of 1969 President Nixon ordered the secret bombing of Cambodia. His goal was to wipe out North Vietnamese and NLF bases along the South Vietnam border. The "Ho Chi Minh trail" went through this area, carrying provisions and troop convoys of the North Vietnamese Army (NVA). When U.S. troops invaded Cambodia the following year, college campuses erupted in protest. Four students at Kent State University in Ohio were killed by national guardsmen who had been called in to prevent rioting. Student protests were staged again in 1971 when the United States provided air support for an ARVN invasion of Laos and in 1972 when the United

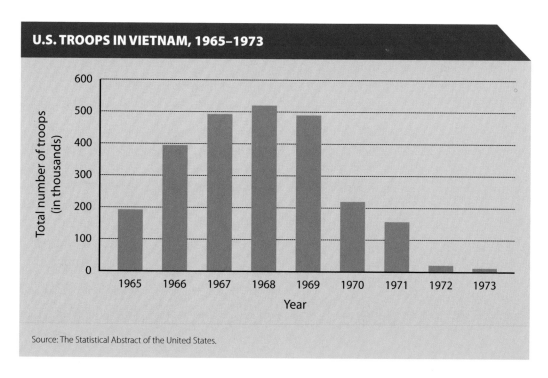

U.S. TROOPS IN VIETNAM, 1965–1973

Source: The Statistical Abstract of the United States.

> On January 27, 1973, U.S. participation in the Vietnam War officially ended when the Treaty of Paris was signed by each of the parties to the conflict.

States began mining the Haiphong harbor. Nixon contended that these operations strengthened his hand at the bargaining table. He pointed to his program of "Vietnamizing" the war, which had reduced the number of U.S. troops in Southeast Asia to under 100,000 by 1972 and gave the South Vietnamese greater control of day-to-day tactical operations. In any event, during Christmas of 1972 the president ordered the final and most intense bombing of the war over Hanoi, the capital of North Vietnam.

On January 27, 1973, U.S. participation in the Vietnam War officially ended when the Treaty of Paris was signed by each of the parties to the conflict. The United States agreed to withdraw all of its forces from Vietnam and stop military operations in Laos and Cambodia. North and South Vietnam agreed to a cease-fire and all prisoners of war were to be released. U.S. military and economic aid to South Vietnam could continue.

Following the collapse of the South Vietnamese regime in 1975, the unified country of Vietnam collectivized the colonial rubber plantations, and some businesses were nationalized. Within ten years, however, elements of capitalism had crept into Vietnamese society. By the 1990s the Vietnam government began instituting policies to bring about a mixed economy involving state, collective, and private ownership. The opening of Vietnamese society improved relations with the United States, which ended a 20-year trade embargo against Vietnam in 1994. Full diplomatic relations between the two countries were established the next year.

Vietnam Seeks Freedom from France Prior to the Vietnam War

Edgar Snow

In the following viewpoint, journalist Edgar Snow explains the precarious position of Vietnam in the year following the end of World War II. Snow describes how France wishes to restore its colonial authority in the region while Vietnamese nationalist forces—backed by China—are coming together in the northern parts of the country to insist on immediate independence. Snow states that this nationalist movement (which includes various Communist groups) is armed and will use force to resist any reassertion of French imperial control. He warns that the United States may be implicated in this showdown because former president Franklin D. Roosevelt promised that all nations would be free from fear of aggression by foreign powers. Silently assenting to French colonial power, Snow suggests, would show the Vietnamese that the United States will not or cannot stand by its words. Edgar Snow was an expert in Chinese affairs and documented the rise of the Chinese Communist Party in his 1937 book *Red Star Over China*.

SOURCE. Edgar Snow, *Saturday Evening Post*, v. 218, February 2, 1946. Copyright © 1946 Saturday Evening Post Society. Reproduced by permission.

It did not take the Japanese to teach the Indo-Chinese to resent French domination or how to struggle for national independence. Fifteen years ago, when I first arrived in Hanoi [Vietnam], the beautiful French-made capital of this richest of all French colonies, I saw an astonishing exhibition, probably typical of many similar lessons in hate.

I was in the lobby of the Hotel Metropole, and the French clerk, an irritable little man from Marseille, had just booked a room for me. He shouted to his Annamite [Vietnamese] porters to carry my bags upstairs. When they did not at once take in his Niagara of French, he strode from behind his desk, grabbed two bewildered Annamites by the back of the neck and repeatedly knocked their skulls together. Civilized men and women of cultured Paris may think I exaggerate, but the hotel was crowded with onlookers who seemed to accept the whole performance as a routine affair.

"They are all children, you know," a French colonial explained over an apéritif, when I recalled the incident. "They have to be disciplined all the time."

Later on, traveling up toward Yünnan on the Tonkin Railway, I saw a French conductor continuing the discipline among native passengers. If one of them was a little slow in surrendering a ticket or said something he considered stupid, this odd character would hand out a routine slap or a re-sounding box on the ears.

Mice Revolting Against the Cats

The Annamites seemed a meek and utterly demoralized people then, but still I could not believe that these sons of an ancient civilization did not have adult pride and dignity behind their dark, unsmiling faces or that they would not soon find ways of demonstrating their wrath. In fact, the French had already been warned by one serious mutiny among Annamite troops in their colonial army in 1929—for the first time in the history of their rule.

Only a year afterward, when I was still in Yünnan, a widespread peasant revolt gave the French another shock. Led by Annamite nationalists who had served with the French in World War I, this agrarian movement raised the usual antilandlord slogans and demands for equal rights and local self-government—in the form of Soviets. It was not so much the degree of danger to the state involved, for the thing was still inchoate nationalism, as it was the very idea that these timid mice would presume to demand anything that excited the French to savage reprisals. They machine-gunned mass meetings of unarmed peasants, bombed their villages, guillotined many of the leaders and rejected all their demands. So one of the most backward colonial administrations in Asia went on unchanged with its civilizing program.

> [The French] machine-gunned mass meetings of unarmed peasants, bombed their villages, guillotined many of the [Vietnamese nationalist] leaders and rejected all their demands.

"We who have lived in France and learned to love and respect her people and her culture are appalled at the chaos and bloodshed we see in our country today," said Mme. Pham Ngoe Thuan, the first Annamite woman admitted to the bar in Indo-China. "We don't hate the French, because we know that here we see only a vicious caricature of the real France," she told me. "But the vast majority of our people know nothing but the oppression, exploitation, discrimination, insults and incompetence of French imperialism, and they have learned to hate everything about it."

Tiny Madame Pham was thin as a blade of grass, and talking to her—like watching the cowering, half-naked captive rebels the French kept squatting all day in the police yard with their hands raised above their heads—gave you again the impression of a nation of mice revolting against the cats. Nevertheless, you sensed, too, a deeper strength of a desperate people goaded beyond endurance, as she continued, "The French could have won our loyalty and gratitude, but their blindness and obstinacy and greed and indifference made them throw away all their chances. After eighty years of French rule, ninety-five per cent of our people still cannot read or write, our splendid resources have not been developed, we have practically no industry, and our per-capita income is less than ten dollars a year. We had nothing resembling self-government, and because of that, we could not defend ourselves against the Japs, and the French did not even try. France may come back with all the force of Allied arms behind her, but her prestige is gone. Our people won't ever again voluntarily submit to French rule."

A New Line-up of Allies

Today, Madame Pham's husband, like many other French-educated Annamite intellectuals, is a rebel official in the newly proclaimed government of an Indo-Chinese republic. And except for a small zone around Saïgon, French power at this writing has ceased to exist throughout a colony which is larger than France itself and contains three fourths as many inhabitants.

> Except for a small zone around Saïgon, French power at this writing has ceased to exist.

Alone, the French might never have got back even to the environs of Saïgon. But with the help, first of all, of American victory in the Pacific, then of the British occupying force, and finally with the aid of the Japanese, the tricolor may eventually be restored in all the main cities of the land—provided the Chinese can be dislodged in the north. What is going on meanwhile is the armed reconquest of a people—just as in Java [Indonesia]—to whom the contradictions of war presented their freedom.

Since the arrival of the British in Saïgon last September third [1945], there has been violence and massacre on both sides, while the Japanese, our erstwhile Fascist enemies, far from being disarmed, have, in fact, become indispensable allies, shooting the natives whom yesterday we promised to liberate.

Here are the Indian colonial troops fighting for the British and against the Annamites, while at home their countrymen demand independence—from a Laborite government now proved no more eager to liquidate the King's empire than its Tory predecessors. Here are the French, themselves lately a conquered people at home, moving their American-armed forces into a lost colony behind an Anglo-Japanese screen of protection.

In Northern Indo-China you have a still more complex picture. Here the troops of Gen. Lu Han are the occupational force in the territory above the sixteenth parallel assigned to the Generalissimo by the Allies—against strenuous French objections. Drawn from the neighboring province of Yünnan, these backwoodsmen are hugely enjoying the not unprofitable task of "disarming the Japanese and restoring law and order." This is Lu Han's reward for tacitly supporting [Chinese nationalist leader] Chiang Kai-shek in a recent coup against Lu Han's uncle, Gen. Lung Yun, whom the Generalissimo finally deposed as warlord dictator of Yünnan last September.

And the Chinese have scores of their own to settle with the French. Northern Indo-China was a Chinese suzerainty until the French detached it in a war fought against China in the last century. Yünnan itself was almost annexed, and for years was a French sphere of influence. Controlling the only railway into Yünnan and its only rail outlet to the sea, the French virtually monopolized Yünnan's foreign trade. Then, in 1940, the Japanese moved in. Complying with their demands, the French closed the railway and thus completed Japan's blockade of China.

China Holds onto the North

So now the Chinese are ready to turn the tables on their neighbors and late Allies. With tens of American-armed divisions and hundreds of American-supplied airplanes behind them, they are demanding control of the railway right through Indo-China to the South China Sea. But if the French demur, the Generalissimo has a trump up his mandarin sleeve. He can always recognize the independent government of Viet Nam—as the Annamite revolutionaries, reviving an ancient name, now call Indo-China.

All of which explains why there was no co-ordination of Chinese policy in the north and Anglo-French policy in the south. Having occupied the northern cities, the Chinese refused to permit the French to fly in their own forces to take over. The paradox was that these same Chinese nationalists were in the north of China itself simultaneously fighting a war—again with American arms—to prevent their own countrymen—Communists, but not foreigners—from doing exactly the same thing they claimed to be doing in Indo-China—that is, "disarming the Japanese and restoring law and order."

Thus, in November, the French in Saïgon still had no direct communications with Hanoi, the capital. Gen. Jacques Leclerc, the able but exasperated *commandant supérieur*, as well as Maj. Gen. Douglas Gracey, Allied CIC [commander-in-chief], had to communicate by way of Ceylon [now Sri Lanka], which relayed their messages to Hanoi through Calcutta and Chungking. Yet Marshal Terauchi, chief of some 120,000 Japanese troops in Indo-China, but himself a prisoner of the British, still had a direct radio circuit to his Hanoi headquarters, which was in contact with Gen. Lu Han. Jap planes were employed by the British for liaison, as well as for bombing and strafing the enemy mice below.

Although in the south any known Annamite revolutionaries were promptly arrested by the British and

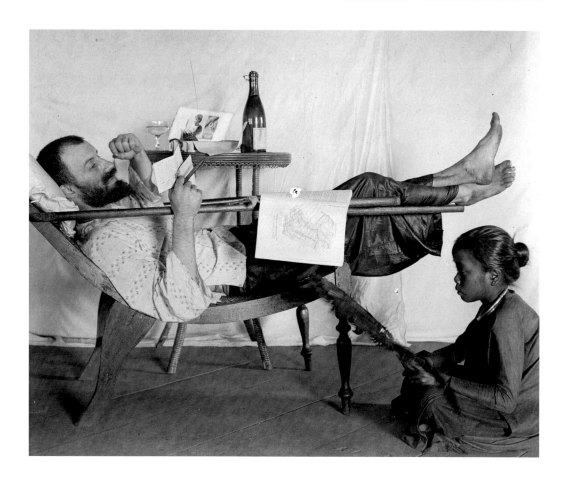

French, in the north the Chinese left native officials in most posts. Ho Chin-minh, president of the provisional government, was invited to the official surrender ceremony of the Japanese in Hanoi, in a city decked with Chinese, Viet Nam and American—but not French—flags.

State buildings everywhere, communications and virtually the whole civil administration were said by the French to remain in rebel hands. The Hanoi radio, which the French repeatedly asked the Chinese to close down, continued to broadcast. Viet Nam's appeals to [U.S. president Harry S.] Truman, [Soviet leader Josef] Stalin, [British prime minister Clement] Attlee, Chiang

Vietnamese people were frequently treated in a subservient manner by French colonialists during the colonial period prior to World War II. (LL/Contributor/ Roger Viollet/Getty Images.)

Kai-shek, the Pope and the world in general, to halt the Anglo-French attempt to reconquer the colony, and bring the whole question before an international arbitration commission or put the country under an international trusteeship. While these exhortations went unanswered by any of the gentlemen addressed, they vexed the French and raised hopes in the breasts of listening Annamites.

The Vietnamese Rebels Remain Armed

Here in Saïgon, the French alleged that many rebels in the new government had been trained in China and even carried Chinese arms. It was known that Chungking had backed a free-Annamite movement during the war and that many of its agents—including President Ho Chin-minh himself—re-entered the country from China. In any event, the Chinese did not disarm the rebels, whose guns were of mixed Japanese, French and British origin—the latter because British planes dropped equipment to guerrillas fighting the Japanese in an earlier stage. Although the Chinese did disarm many Japanese, they apparently interfered little with some Japanese who had joined the rebels. Nor did they prevent the influx of Japanese whom the Siamese [Thai], permitted to escape across their border.

Such was the complicated, many-colored mosaic which confronted the new French government this past December. General Gracey, a tough-fibered British Tory with no sentimentality about him, frankly admitted that there was no immediate prospect of disarming the Japs or of restoring French power. Only a campaign of long duration, "many months" at least, could undo the mischief. And envoys from "the new France," at first optimistic because they brought well-intentioned promises of reform and "complete self-government" which they had thought eminently fair, rapidly turned pessimistic as they realized that nothing short of a guarantee of independence could now furnish a basis for peaceful settlement. Bitterly they blamed the whole catastrophe on the pro-Fascist, reactionary colonial administration of the past.

> About 98 per cent of the Annamites sympathize with the demand for full independence.

The fact, as nearly as neutral observers could ascertain, is that about 98 per cent of the Annamites sympathize with the demand for full independence. And Annamites, according to M. Fischbercher, head of the French Information Service, account for 23,000,000 of the nation's 28,000,000 inhabitants—the remainder, largely Cambodian and Lao peoples, making up a separate minority problem. Whether any of these millions are really ready for independence is a horse of a different color.

France's Bid to Retain Colonial Control

French arguments against throwing in the sponge now run about as follows: First, they still insist that only a small percentage of the population is against them. Secondly, the Viet Nam government was set up and armed by the Japanese; it co-operated with the enemy. Third, the Annamites—or Viet Namites—are uneducated children who could never run a government without French supervision. Fourth, the republic could never stand; it could not defend itself against Siam and China, both of whom are described by the French as "aggressive states." Fifth, continued French rule is also necessary, as Admiral Thierry d'Argenlieu, chief of civil affairs, points out, "in order to protect the minorities against Annamite imperialism."

But facts of recent history seem to vitiate the validity of all those contentions. It is true that some Annamite nationalists worked with the Japanese, but the French began the practice. As for stability of a native regime, the French themselves admit that the present administration in the interior consists of almost exactly the same bureaucracy that formerly served for them. Even before the war was over, 90 per cent of the government workers were natives and the whole French community numbered about 40,000.

However confused its political character, the revolutionary government was sufficiently influential to enforce a virtually complete boycott of Saïgon after it was seized by the Allies, when 95 per cent of the natives abandoned the city. The French could not get a single Annamite to attend their first conference of civil-government officials. Possibly China and Siam would gobble up the new state, but France proved unable to defend it against the Japanese and thereby failed to fulfill her obligations to her protectorate. Annamites think they could do better at saving themselves from their neighbors without the presence of French power.

Even French claims to represent the interests of the minorities appear to be largely self-asserted. Although Cambodians are not taking active part in the Viet Nam government, the puppet king secretly sympathized with it and hoped to secure independence for his own state through its success. British paratroopers were already on the spot, however, occupying the king's capital, famed Phnom Penh, when they learned of a plot. They arrested some of the recalcitrant puppets, including the prime minister, whom they flew down to Saïgon, where the jails were already crowded with Annamites. A similar fate overtook the prime minister's successor.

> It became obvious that the most potent argument for restoration of French power was the necessity to preserve the whole colonial system.

As for the little kingdom in the Laos territory, which is ruled by a dynasty created by the French, there, also, no welcome mat was out for the return of the white gods. The Annamites offered the Laos territory state autonomy within a federation, and the king watchfully waited. In answer to French appeals for aid, he disarmed and interned all Frenchmen—"for their own protection."

Thus it became obvious that the most potent argument for restoration of French power was the necessity to preserve the whole colonial system, for the collapse of one pillar weakens the whole edifice. The question of Indo-China's readiness for independence would not be answered by theses built on moral grounds or the logic of justice. Nor would it be settled in this new era of "American world leadership" in accordance with President Truman's fourth commandment of foreign policy "that all peoples who are prepared for self-government should be permitted to choose their own form of government . . . without interference from any foreign sources . . . in Asia . . . as well as in the Western Hemisphere."

If Revolution Comes to Viet Nam

Rather, it may be determined, as issues of slavery versus freedom have always been settled in the past, by the sum of armed force the slaves are able to mobilize, by the degree of fanaticism with which they resist, by the moral and political strength behind their struggle and, in the last resort, by the preparedness of the revolutionaries not so much for self-government as to be machine-gunned, bombed or perhaps atomized in defense of their inalienable rights as free men.

And if such is the case, what are the Annamites' chances of success? The answer may lie in tracing the history of the revolution which began with the peasant rebellion of 1930. It had the backing of Annamite nationalists strongly influenced by their reading of French history, but even more by the Chinese revolution and by the Filipinos' successful campaign for independence. Among its leaders also were Annam's first Communists, who for a time had connections with the Comintern [international communist organization headquartered in Moscow]. Driven underground, these nationalists built up some following in the villages until 1936, when there was a reform movement in the colony led by Léon Blum's Popular-Front government.

This period promised to reconcile antagonisms in a progressive evolution toward democratic self-government. But it was as brief-lived as Blum's Front Populaire, and under [French prime minister Edouard] Daladier all such moves were halted or put into reverse. Both nationalists and Communists were again suppressed, and scores were arrested. Working underground once more, the native leaders turned more radical in their demands and began to infiltrate the French-officered army. When, after the fall of France, the Vichyite [pro-Fascist] governor-general, Admiral Decoux, negotiated a treaty permitting the Japanese to make a base of Indo-China, there was an insurrection in the army which lasted well into 1941. It was put down by the joint efforts of the Japanese and the French Foreign Legion. . . .

Meanwhile, the defeated Annamite insurrectionists had fallen back on the villages and begun to organize an armed underground—for a time assisted by a few French Communists. In 1942, the left-wing Nationalists and Communists formed a National Front and recruited numerous partisans in the rural districts. Finally, in March, 1945, having exhausted the usefulness of the French administration and anxious to win some aid from the Annamites in the expected battle for Indo-China, the Japanese dissolved the Decoux government, disarmed the French troops and interned all Frenchmen. At the same time they set up an "independent" government of conservative Annamite nationalists and sought to win over some of the more anti-French guerrillas.

The Jap-organized regime was succeeded by the present provisional government of Viet Nam, which came to power immediately following V-J day. It resulted from a fusion between the Communists, who appear to have the more effective organization but are divided into different factions, and the various groups of nationalists, which formed a coalition known as the Viet Minh Party. The Japanese offered little opposition when the revolutionary regime was set up on August seventeenth, headed by the nationalist leader, Ho Chin-minh, as president, and by Nguyen Aiquo, a founder of the Annamite Communist party, as premier. Dr. P.N. Thach, leader of the Viet Minh Youth Vanguard Party and a moderate nationalist, became Minister of Foreign Affairs. All three men, as most of the rest of the cabinet, are French-educated—although Ho Chin-minh spent ten years as an exile in Russia and China.

The Japanese withdrew from all public buildings and the Viet Nam government took over effective control of the country, with its capital at Hanoi, and a southern-branch government in Saïgon. It proclaimed itself a democratic republic and asked for admission to the United Nations Organization, which it requested to supervise a plebiscite and national election.

> When British troops reached Saïgon in September [1945] the city was in the hands of the Annamites.

Fighting in Saïgon

Thus, when British troops reached Saïgon in September the city was in the hands of the Annamites. Dr. Thach negotiated with General Gracey and rather naïvely agreed to let the British enter the country unopposed, on the understanding that their sole mission was to disarm the Japanese and preserve law and order. Once installed, Gracey immediately ordered the Japanese troops to return to their posts, and they came out of their barracks and began to resume police power in Saïgon. The British commander then rearmed the 11th French Regiment, which had formerly helped the Japanese police in Indo-China, but were interned by them last March.

> *Despite its strong Communist influence, the Viet Nam government's announced program is that of a purely bourgeois Nationalist independence movement.*

Backed by Gracey's Indians and the Japanese, the 4,000 ex-Vichyite French troops then attempted to take over all the public buildings and oust the Annamite officials—a move which the native forces finally resisted with guns. Outnumbered, outgunned and outwitted, they were forced to retreat. By mid-October when General Leclerc's 2nd Armored Division finally began to arrive, the British had 24,000 troops in Saïgon and the Annamites had been pushed back to the outskirts of the city. A perimeter was set up preparatory to a major offensive against the revolutionaries in the interior.

America had no troops in Saïgon, but was represented by a small staff of OSS [Office of Strategic Services] officers and noncoms whose presence afforded the Air Transport Command a *raison d'être* [reason] for operations which could later be converted into commercial airline rights. During the battle for Saïgon, an American OSS officer, Lt. Col. A. Peter Dewey, in a jeep near the airfield, was ambushed and killed by unidentified Annamites.

Unfortunately, only a short time before the incident, General Gracey had ordered all American flags removed from our transport and equipment in this area, and subsequent investigation by OSS led them to the conclusion that the attack was a case of mistaken identity.

Flags were restored on American vehicles next day and there were no more incidents. But the French quickly realized the propaganda value of the tragedy, and announced that they would not discuss matters with Annamite delegates any further unless Dewey's body was brought to them. The Viet Nam government offered a reward of 5,000 piastres for the corpse, and presumably conducted a fruitless search—and negotiations are still suspended at this writing.

The Composition of the Nationalist Forces

Despite its strong Communist influence, the Viet Nam government's announced program is that of a purely bourgeois Nationalist independence movement. Its connections with China are with Chiang Kai-shek's nationalists rather than the Communists, and the French scoff at any suggestion of Russian interest in its fate. French Communists in Saïgon were advisers of Viet Nam leaders until hostilities began, but later adopted an equivocal position. They blamed both the Annamites, for lack of faith in the good intentions of a "new France" in which Communists would have much to say about colonial policy, and the [French provisional president Charles] De Gaulle government, for refusing to use the word "independence" in its offers to the rebels.

Annamite forces were estimated at about 180,000, poorly trained and poorly armed—some of them with bows and arrows and native swords. But they also include French-trained Annamite officers and about 8,000 Japanese deserters—who were being shot at once on capture. The composition of the movement is extremely heterogeneous, ranging from pirates, semi-bandit groups and obscure religious sects to highly educated, westernized intellectuals in control of a nucleus of disciplined troops. Thousands of rebels have already been killed in preliminary skirmishes in which natives have sometimes fought with fanatical courage against great odds. Though the French have all the advantages of modern arms and transport, this looked like a real social revolution pushed forward by the masses and rapidly expanding. The leaders were unlikely to surrender as long as they had hopes of holding power in the north under Chinese occupancy.

Much depended on the policy adopted by the French government following the recent elections. An offer of independence at a definite date and a comprehensive program of education for self-government, coupled with planned economic and social development, might yet make a compromise possible, avoid further bloodshed and intensification of race hatred and save Indo-China for the French Empire, for a while at least. Moderate and conservative Annamites both told me that all but a minority of extremists would probably lay down their arms in response to such a declaration.

"What the people really want is a solemn guarantee of independence in the near future, such as the United States made to the Philippines," I was told by Madame Thach, the French wife of the Viet Nam foreign minister. "Most educated Annamites realize that they still need European help to develop the country. They would be glad to have France furnish the technicians and advisers, if she could only do so on a basis of equality."

Looking to the United States

But few Annamites seemed ready to believe in any such change of heart in the French. Instead, millions built their hopes on the United States—odd as it may sound to you. "The victory in the Pacific is yours," many came to me and said. "It was you and not the French who defeated the Japanese. Why do you have no voice in how the victory is used here?"

They had listened to our own and Chinese radio broadcasts all during the war, and they heard the speeches about a brave new world of United Nations of free peoples sent out from San Francisco. Now they could not understand that we really did not mean the Four Freedoms[1] to apply to Annamites, too, nor that President Truman had no plan to impose his twelve commandments of foreign policy in the French colonies. They could not see why we contend that Bulgaria and Romania are ready for self-government and we insist upon "free democratic elections" in those nations which fought for [Nazi German leader Adolf] Hitler, while we maintain silence when the Annamites, who never joined the Axis, demand the same rights.

This is one of the reasons why some observers out here keep saying that America ended the war with greater prestige than any nation in history—and is losing it more rapidly than any nation in history.

Note

1. In 1941, President Franklin D. Roosevelt declared that all people had four fundamental freedoms: freedom of speech, freedom of religion, freedom from want, and freedom from fear. These freedoms were incorporated into the United Nations' Declaration of Human Rights in 1948.

South Vietnam Struggles to Rebuild After Partition

Economist

In the viewpoint that follows, the *Economist*, a British journal that avoids author bylines so that the magazine may speak with one unified voice, assesses the leadership of Ngo Dinh Diem in his first eight months in office as president of South Vietnam. According to the *Economist*, Diem has inherited a lackluster economy and a divided populace—some favoring the Communist Viet Minh forces that hold the North and others content to share the fortunes of the free republic in the South. Although faced with such pressing problems—including the fact that his republic exists only as a result of the temporary partition of Vietnam that began in 1954, the magazine portrays Diem as an official impressed with the pomp of his office rather than the concerns of his nation. The *Economist* sees the appointment of a new minister of economics, Nguyen Ngoc Tho, as a step in the right direction for South Vietnam's ailing economy,

SOURCE. "Diem's Shaky Foundations," *Economist*, vol. 179, June 23, 1956, pp. 45–46. Reproduced by permission.

but it warns that fixing markets will not be enough to pacify a nation still largely crying out for reunification.

Acertain complacency appears to have settled on the West about South Vietnam's future. The belief seems to be gaining ground that everything is going swimmingly south of the 17th parallel, that President Ngo Dinh Diem has communist infiltration well in hand, and that, now the Anglo-Russian talks in London have got round the snag of the elections originally scheduled for this July [1946], the Vietnamese problem can be quietly shelved. The ultimate fate of the country depends, however, not on conference tables in distant capitals, but on the internal ferment in Vietnam itself—and particularly in the south where, despite the simplification caused by the defeat of the rebel sects and the departure of the French expeditionary corps, much is still fluid.

Looking at South Vietnam Optimistically and Pessimistically

The drama of South Vietnam lies in the fact that it provides the most immediate test of whether the American aid programme can do what it is intended to do—to diminish and finally master communist infiltration in poverty-stricken Asia. Unfortunately, to arrive at the truth about the present situation in South Vietnam is almost as difficult in Saigon as it is in London or Paris. Almost all sources of information in South Vietnam are tainted, in the sense that they are divided between those who are determined to be optimists and those who are equally determined to be pessimists. With exceptions, the optimists consist of the government and civil service, the entire Vietnamese press, the American aid missions, and the American and British embassies. The pessimists comprise the French, together with the enemies of the present regime and (it must be admitted) a considerable

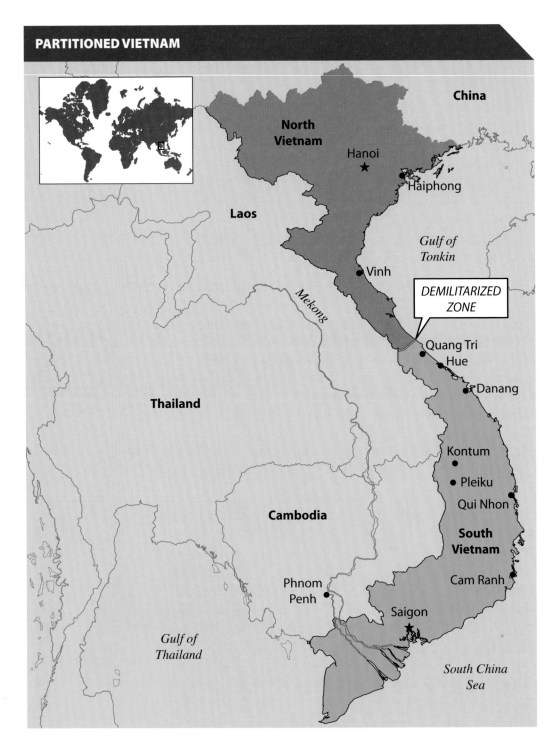

PARTITIONED VIETNAM

China

North
Vietnam

Hanoi
★

Haiphong

Laos

Gulf of
Tonkin

Vinh

Mekong

DEMILITARIZED
ZONE

Quang Tri
Hue

Danang

Thailand

Kontum

Pleiku

Qui Nhon

Cambodia

South
Vietnam

Phnom
Penh

Cam Ranh

Saigon
★

Gulf of
Thailand

South China
Sea

number of independent observers. It is extremely difficult even to get answers to questions of fact—how many refugees have actually been settled on the land, how well advanced the agrarian reform programme is, how much the pacification in west Cochin-China [the region encompassing Saigon] has improved the rice-growing prospects, and, most important of all, what the real degree of communist infiltration is in the south.

The optimists maintain that the problem of dealing with infiltration is now well in hand. They claim that purges in the Army and civil service have been thorough; that recantations or arrests of Viet Minh [Communists] have been numerous and that the people are steadily rallying to the government; and that victory over the sects has been a conclusive blow to the Viet Minh, who were using them for their own ends. The pessimists reply that infiltration in the high plateaux of Central Annam [Vietnam] via the Laotian frontier has never been more serious; that areas such as the Camau in the far south have never really abandoned their allegiance to the Viet Minh; that the defeat of the sects has profited the Viet Minh, since the latter have taken over the rank and file abandoned by their leaders, thereby replacing open rebellion by clandestine subversion; that the administration is riddled, if not with communist agents, at best with timeservers who would work for any regime; and, finally, that the peasant in the ricefields tends to regard Uncle Ho [Ho Chi Minh] rather than Mr. Diem as the architect of national independence.

> Those who have watched [Ngo Dinh Diem] closely are beginning to doubt whether he has enough of the qualities of a popular leader.

Assessing Diem's Character

It must be remembered that the only press agency in Saigon, from which a large proportion of the news from the

> It is sometimes forgotten that if South Vietnam does not compete, economically and socially, with the north, it is in the long run doomed.

south originates, is not independent but an almost open organ of governmental propaganda. Furthermore, no opposition newspaper exists in South Vietnam and there are few foreign correspondents left in Saigon. The result is that most of the information now going out—especially to London and Washington—tends to have an optimistic note. To say this is not to deny the striking successes gained recently by Mr. Diem. His principal achievement has been to defeat the sects, and the names of Cao Dai [a religious sect that established its own private army], Hoa Hao [a Buddhist religion], and Binh Xuyen [a private army of racketeers and smugglers working within the Vietnamese Nationalist Army] no longer burden the international telegrams. It is very easy to underestimate Mr. Diem. This time last year he had very few convinced backers; now he has won prestige and authority, even among his critics. He is known, and feared, in his country. He combines the skilful inactivity of [former British prime minister Stanley] Baldwin with the obstinacy of [French general Charles] de Gaulle. He is as incorruptible as [eighteenth-century French revolutionary Maximilien] Robespierre.

Yet those who have watched him closely are beginning to doubt whether he has enough of the qualities of a popular leader. His ceremonial tours in the provinces are full of formal speeches and presentations and docile village deputations upon whom he confers his benediction, in the manner of pope or emperor rather than of revolutionary leader. He has been compared to Dr. [Antonio de Oliveira] Salazar of Portugal, but the comparison fails in two important ways. Dr. Salazar is a professor of economics; Diem is very much not. And Salazar does not have a crafty, ruthless, and long-sighted enemy immediately across his frontier.

South Vietnam's Weak Economy

Certain political aspects of Diem's regime are unsatisfactory. There is too little freedom, and it is doubtful whether this is justified by any corresponding increase in efficiency. But the crux of the matter is the economic situation. Until now the government has tended to recline upon the easy sofa of American economic aid. The fact that almost the entire import programme of South Vietnam is financed by this aid is not surprising; it can be regarded as an inevitable aftermath of the long war which devastated the rich ricefields on which Vietnam's prewar export trade depended. The cumbrous mechanism by which the aid process functions, adding about four months to normal delivery periods, is perhaps difficult to improve. More serious, and presumably more avoidable, are the abuses—the sales of foreign currency, the illegal traffic in licences, the indirect marketing of goods to the Viet Minh, the stocking or hoarding by undesirable intermediaries which prevents essential things from reaching the people who need them, and other practices which have diminished the efficacity, and also the reputation, of this great experiment. By far the most pungent criticism of the programme as it stands is that it seems calculated to do little more than supply the consumer goods which the Vietnamese, lacking foreign currency, cannot buy for themselves, instead of helping them to restore their productive apparatus at a rate which can compete with communist-aided North Vietnam.

> It is indeed doubtful how long a [South Vietnamese] policy which practically slams the door on unification can be maintained.

The principal items of the aid programme to South Vietnam for the next six months are condensed milk, flour, sugar, petrol and oil, bicycles and motor scooters, textiles, tobacco, and cement. It is sometimes forgotten that if South Vietnam does not compete, economically and socially, with the north, it is in the long run doomed. Admittedly, it is difficult suddenly to start importing industrial machinery, schools, hospitals, trained technicians, skilled labour, and foreign capital; and it is only too easy to criticise what is being done in these countries by American aid administrators, whose enthusiasm and skill in their difficult job are perhaps the most important contribution under their own aid programme. But the problem facing Mr. Diem is urgent.

A New Minister of Economics

The steadily falling value of the southern piastre [currency] reflects the economic malaise of South Vietnam. Inflation is rampant, transfers of capital out of the country have reached indecent proportions, and unemployment is calculated at 300,000 out of a population of 11 million. Much, however, may depend on the performance of the new minister of economics, Mr. Nguyen Ngoc Tho, an able man who recently served as ambassador in Tokyo. Mr. Tho has made an excellent first impression and has already shown that he is willing to take the kind of drastic measures the situation demands. On June 13th, for instance, he announced new import regulations which should reduce the volume of unnecessary imports and discourage illegal use or transfers of import licences. Admittedly the overriding problem for Vietnam is not an economic but a political one—unification—and this is never long absent from the conversation of Vietnamese intellectuals. It is indeed doubtful how long a policy which practically slams the door on unification can be maintained. But if, as now seems possible, division is prolonged, it is highly desirable that the economic aid programme to the south should no longer be limited to a light sprinkling of useful commodities, but should start the process of reconstruction.

It has to be remembered that the Viet Minh enjoys the lustre of having fought for and achieved national in-

Photo on opposite page: The falling value of the South Vietnamese currency helped exacerbate a weak economy and widespread poverty throughout the country. (Wilbur E. Garrett/ National Geographic/ Getty Images.)

dependence, and of having defeated the French army in the field. Radical changes, both economic and political, are needed if the south is to hold its own. President Diem may be a big enough man to carry them out. But if he does not, then it is to [Chinese nationalist leader] General Chiang Kai-shek in the fateful days of 1947 and 1948 [when Chiang was first elected president of the Republic of China but immediately faced communist opposition that ended his reign in 1949], rather than to Dr. Salazar, that he will one day be compared.

The President of South Vietnam Appeals to the United States for Aid Against North Vietnam

Ngo Dihn Diem

Ngo Dinh Diem served as the first president of the Republic of Vietnam (South Vietnam). He came to power after Vietnam was partitioned in 1954, following the defeat of the French military in its bid to retain control of the former colony. Diem seized the reins of government after fraudulent elections and cast his lot with the United States, not France, hoping that U.S. support would keep him in power as a valuable ally against Communist incursion from the North. Washington kept friendly relations with Diem for just that reason, but the U.S. government put no faith in Diem's regime, which was known for corruption and intolerance. In 1961, Diem wrote a letter to President John F. Kennedy, ensuring South Vietnam's commitment to peace but worrying over insurgent attacks by Communist forces (Viet Cong) in the

---

SOURCE. Ngo Dihn Diem, "The President of South Vietnam Appeals to the United States for Aid against North Vietnam," presidency.ucsb. edu. Reproduced by permission.

South that have plunged the country into a state of war. The following viewpoint reproduces the text of that letter. Claiming that his own defense troops are too few to thwart the enemy, Diem calls on the U.S. president to provide "further assistance" to help stem the Communist tide. Washington had been supplying weapons and military "advisors" to South Vietnam since the 1950s, but Kennedy saw Diem's plea as a means to significantly increase U.S. troop levels and take a more active hand in protecting the South from hostile takeover. The aid did not hold back the Communists, and once Diem's military strategy and social programs began to seriously compromise the security of the region, Kennedy's administration did nothing to stop a South Vietnamese military coup from assassinating Diem and overthrowing his regime in early November 1963.

D ear Mr. President:
Since its birth, more than six years ago, the Republic of Viet-Nam has enjoyed the close friendship and cooperation of the United States of America.

Like the United States, the Republic of Viet-Nam has always been devoted to the preservation of peace. My people know only too well the sorrows of war. We have honored the 1954 Geneva Agreements even though they resulted in the partition of our country and the enslavement of more than half of our people by Communist tyranny. We have never considered the reunification of our nation by force. On the contrary, we have publicly pledged that we will not violate the demarcation line and the demilitarized zone set up by the agreements. We have always been prepared and have on many occasions stated our willingness to reunify Viet-Nam on the basis of democratic and truly free elections.

The record of the Communist authorities in the northern part of our country is quite otherwise. They not only consented to the division of Viet-Nam, but were eager for it. They pledged themselves to observe the Geneva Agreements and during the seven years since have never ceased to violate them. They call for free elections but are ignorant of the very meaning of the words. They talk of "peaceful reunification" and wage war against us.

Communist Plans to Overthrow Democracy

From the beginning, the Communists resorted to terror in their efforts to subvert our people, destroy our government, and impose a Communist regime upon us. They have attacked defenseless teachers, closed schools, killed members of our anti-malarial program, and looted hospitals. This is coldly calculated to destroy our government's humanitarian efforts to serve our people.

> From the beginning, the Communists resorted to terror in their efforts to subvert our people, destroy our government, and impose a Communist regime upon us.

We have long sought to check the Communist attack from the North on our people by appeals to the International Control Commission [ICC, which oversaw the partition of Vietnam and the subsequent ceasefire between North and South]. Over the years, we have repeatedly published to the world the evidence of the Communist plot to overthrow our government and seize control of all of Viet-Nam by illegal intrusions from outside our country. The evidence has mounted until now it is hardly necessary to rehearse it. Most recently, the kidnapping and brutal murder of our Chief Liaison Officer to the International Control Commission, Colonel Noang Thuy Nam, compelled us to speak out once more. In our October 24, 1961, letter to the ICC, we called attention again to the publicly stated determination of the Communist authorities in Hanoi to "liberate the South" by the overthrow of my government and the imposition of a Communist regime on our people. We cited the proof of massive infiltration of Com-

South Vietnamese president Ngo Dinh Diem (center) appealed to U.S. president John F. Kennedy for support in defeating the Vietcong and North Vietnamese Communists. (Wilbur E. Garrett/Contributor/ National Geographic/ Getty Images.)

munist agents and military elements into our country. We outlined the Communist strategy, which is simply the ruthless use of terror against the whole population, women and children included.

In the course of the last few months, the Communist assault on my people has achieved high ferocity. In October they caused more than 1,800 incidents of violence and more than 2,000 casualties. They have struck occasionally in battalion strength, and they are continually augmenting their forces by infiltration from the North.

The level of their attacks is already such that our forces are stretched to the utmost. We are forced to defend every village, every hamlet, indeed every home against a foe whose tactic is always to strike at the defenseless.

A disastrous flood was recently added to the misfortunes of the Vietnamese people. The greater part of three provinces was inundated, with a great loss of property. We are now engaged in a nationwide effort to reconstruct and rehabilitate this area. The Communists are, of course, making this task doubly difficult, for they have seized upon the disruption of normal administration and communications as an opportunity to sow more destruction in the stricken area.

> We are forced to defend every village, every hamlet, indeed every home against a foe whose tactic is always to strike at the defenseless.

Help Save Our National Soul

In short, the Vietnamese nation now faces what is perhaps the gravest crisis in its long history. For more than 2,000 years my people have lived and built, fought and died in this land. We have not always been free. Indeed, much of our history and many of its proudest moments have arisen from conquest by foreign powers and our struggle against great odds to regain or defend our precious independence. But it is not only our freedom which is at stake today, it is our national identity. For, if we lose this war, our people will be swallowed by the Communist Bloc, all our proud heritage will be blotted out by the "Socialist society," and Viet-Nam will leave the pages of history. We will lose our national soul.

Mr. President, my people and I are mindful of the great assistance which the United States has given us. Your help has not been lightly received, for the Vietnamese are proud people, and we are determined to do our part in the defense of the free world. It is clear to all of us that the defeat of the Viet Cong demands the total mobilization of our government and our people, and you may be sure that we will devote all of our resources of money, minds, and men to this great task.

But Viet-Nam is not a great power and the forces of International Communism now arrayed against us are more than we can meet with the resources at hand. We must have further assistance from the United States if we are to win the war now being waged against us.

We can certainly assure mankind that our action is purely defensive. Much as we regret the subjugation of more than half our people in North Viet-Nam, we have

The Viet Cong

The common term for the Communist guerrillas of South Vietnam [was the "Viet Cong"]. The term, meaning simply "Vietnamese Communists," was slightly derogatory and was first used by Ngo Dinh Diem, president of South Vietnam from 1955 to 1963, in his effort to identify a challenge he never took seriously. The Viet Cong [VC] evolved from the southern remnant of the Viet Minh forces left after the First Indochina War (1946–1954). Their number was small, probably fewer than ten thousand, and they were joined by disaffected members of the Hoa Hao, Cao Dai, and Binh Xuyen armies as well as others who had little love for the Diem regime. . . .

Officially, the VC was the National Front for the Liberation of South Vietnam, or, more familiarly, the National Liberation Front (NLF). VC fighters, for their part, were organized into the People's Liberation Armed Forces (PLAF). Both organizations were officially formed in December 1960. The NLF took on the tasks of education, recruitment, and policy coordination with Hanoi while the PLAF began a guerrilla war against Diem's regime almost immediately.

SOURCE. *Jeff T. Hay, "Viet Cong," The Greenhaven Encyclopedia of the Vietnam War. Ed. Charles Zappia. San Diego: Greenhaven, 2004.*

no intention, and indeed no means, to free them by use of force.

I have said that Viet-Nam is at war. War means many things, but most of all it means the death of brave people for a cause they believe in. Viet-Nam has suffered many wars, and through the centuries we have always had patriots and heroes who were willing to shed their blood for Viet-Nam. We will keep faith with them.

When Communism has long ebbed away into the past, my people will still be here, a free united nation growing from the deep roots of our Vietnamese heritage. They will remember your help in our time of need. This struggle will then be a part of our common history. And your help, your friendship, and the strong bonds between our two peoples will be a part of Viet-Nam, then as now.

Ngo Dihn Diem

The United States Pledges to Support South Vietnam in Its Quest to Remain Free

Robert S. McNamara

Robert S. McNamara served as the U.S. secretary of defense under presidents John F. Kennedy and Lyndon Johnson. He was a chief planner of U.S. strategy in the Vietnam War. In the following viewpoint, an excerpt from a speech given to the National Security Industrial Association in 1964, McNamara outlines why U.S. aid to Vietnam is necessary. He contends that the United States is committed to helping all nations that struggle for freedom against Communist takeover and that thwarting communism's involvement in so-called wars of liberation will deny the Soviet Union and China from infiltrating and manipulating the politics of key global regions. McNamara argues that South Vietnam under General Nguyen Khanh is a valuable U.S. ally

SOURCE. Robert S. McNamara, "South Vietnam: The United States Policy," delivered at the James Forrestal Memorial Awards dinner of the National Security Industrial Association, Washington, D.C., March 26, 1964.

that only needs U.S. aid to strengthen its own defenses against Communist aggression from the North. He maintains that they can contain that threat if the United States helps reorganize the South Vietnamese army and supplies it with weapons to defend itself. While Khanh's government received the aid it needed, the South Vietnamese army could not cope with a better trained and motivated enemy. Roughly a year after McNamara's speech, Lyndon Johnson would commit the first U.S. combat troops to Vietnam.

This evening I want to discuss South Vietnam with you. In South Vietnam, as you well know, the independence of a nation and the freedom of its people are being threatened by Communist aggression and terrorism. In response to requests from the Government of South Vietnam, the United States since 1954 has been providing assistance to the Vietnamese in their struggle to maintain their independence. . . .

> "The Vietnamese have asked for our help. We have given it. We shall continue to give it."

America's Objectives

Our concern is threefold.

First, and most important, is the simple fact that South Vietnam, a member of the free world family, is striving to preserve its independence from Communist attack. The Vietnamese have asked for our help. We have given it. We shall continue to give it.

We do so in their interest; and we do so in our own clear self-interest. For basic to the principles of freedom and self-determination which have sustained our country for almost two centuries is the right of peoples everywhere to live and develop in peace.

Our own security is strengthened by the determination of others to remain free, and by our commitment to assist them. We will not let this member of our family down, regardless of its distance from our shores.

The ultimate goal of the United States in Southeast Asia, as in the rest of the world, is to help maintain free and independent nations which can develop politically, economically and socially, and which can be responsible members of the world community.

In this region and elsewhere, many peoples share our sense of the value of such freedom and independence. They have taken the risks and made the sacrifices linked to the commitment to membership in the family of the free world.

> "Southeast Asia has great strategic significance in the forward defense of the United States."

They have done this in the belief that we would back up our pledges to help defend them. It is not right or even expedient—nor is it in our nature—to abandon them when the going is difficult.

Second, Southeast Asia has great strategic significance in the forward defense of the United States. Its location across east-west air and sea lanes flanks the Indian subcontinent on one side and Australia, New Zealand, and the Philippines on the other, and dominates the gateway between the Pacific and Indian Oceans.

In Communist hands this area would pose a most serious threat to the security of the United States and to the family of free world nations to which we belong. To defend Southeast Asia we must meet the challenge in South Vietnam.

A New Communist Strategy

And third, South Vietnam is a test case for the new Communist strategy. Let me examine for a moment the nature of this strategy.

As the [John F.] Kennedy Administration was coming into office in January, 1961, [Soviet] Chairman [Nikita] Khrushchev made one of the most important speeches on Communist strategy of recent decades. In his report on a party conference entitled "For New Victories of the World Communist Movement, Khrushchev stated: "In modern conditions, the following categories of wars should be distinguished: world wars, local wars, liberation wars and popular uprisings."

He ruled out what he called "world wars" and "local wars" as being too dangerous for profitable indulgence in a world of nuclear weapons. But with regard to what he called "liberation wars," he referred specifically to Vietnam. He said, "It is a sacred war. We recognize such wars."

I have pointed out on other occasions the enormous strategic nuclear power which the United States has developed to cope with the first of Mr. Khrushchev's types of wars; deterrence of deliberate, calculated nuclear attack seems as assured as it can be.

With respect to our general purpose forces designed especially for local wars, within the past three years we have increased the number of our combat-ready army divisions by about 45 per cent, tactical air squadrons by 30 per cent, airlift capabilities by 75 per cent, with a 100 per cent increase in ship construction and conversion.

> Today in Vietnam we are not dealing with factional disputes or the remnants of a colonial struggle against the French, but rather with a major test case of Communism's new strategy.

In conjunction with the forces of our allies, our global posture for deterrence and defense is still not all that it should be, but it is good.

President Kennedy and President [Lyndon] Johnson have recognized, however, that our forces for the first two types of wars might not be applicable or effective against what the Communists call "wars of liberation," or what is properly called covert aggression or insurgency.

We have therefore undertaken and continue to press a variety of programs to develop skilled specialists, equipment, and techniques to enable us to help our allies counter the threat of insurgency.

Communist interest in insurgency techniques did not begin with Khrushchev, nor for that matter with [Soviet leader Josef] Stalin. [Russian revolutionary Vladimir] Lenin's works are full of tactical instructions, which were adapted very successfully by [Chinese Communist leader] Mao Tse-tung, whose many writings on guerrilla warfare have become classic references.

Indeed, Mao claims to be the true heir of Lenin's original prescriptions for the worldwide victory of Communism. The North Vietnamese have taken a leaf or two from Mao's book—as well as Moscow's—and added some of their own.

A Region Ripe for Communist Insurgency and Conquest

Thus today in Vietnam we are not dealing with factional disputes or the remnants of a colonial struggle against the French, but rather with a major test case of Communism's new strategy. That strategy has so far been pursued in Cuba, may be beginning in Africa, and failed in Malaya and the Philippines only because of a long and arduous struggle by the people of these countries with assistance provided by the British and the United States.

In Southeast Asia the Communists have taken full advantage of geography—the proximity to the Communist base of operations and the rugged, remote and heavily foliated character of the border regions.

They have utilized the diverse ethnic, religious, and tribal groupings, and exploited factionalism and legitimate aspirations wherever possible. And, as I said earlier, they have resorted to sabotage, terrorism, and assassination on an unprecedented scale.

Who is the responsible party—the prime aggressor? First and foremost, without doubt, the prime aggressor is North Vietnam, whose leadership has explicitly un-

A Vietcong guerrilla is interrogated by a member of the South Vietnamese military. U.S. secretary of defense Robert McNamara cited the 60,000 to 80,000 Vietcong guerrillas as a threat sufficient to warrant U.S. intervention. (Larry Burrows/ Contributor/Time & Life Pictures/Getty Images.)

dertaken to destroy the independence of the south. To be sure, Hanoi is encouraged on its aggressive course by Communist China. But Peiping's [now Beijing] interest is hardly the same as that of Hanoi.

For Hanoi the immediate objective is limited: conquest of the south and national unification, perhaps coupled with control of Laos. For Peiping, however, Hanoi's victory would be only a first step toward eventual Chinese hegemony over the two Vietnams and Southeast Asia, and toward exploitation of the new strategy in other parts of the world.

Communist China's interests are clear: it has publicly castigated Moscow for betraying the revolutionary cause whenever the Soviets have sounded a cautionary note. It has characterized the United States as a paper tiger and has insisted that the revolutionary struggle for "liberation and unification" of Vietnam could be conducted without risks by, in effect, crawling under the nuclear and the conventional defense of the free world.

Peiping thus appears to feel that it has a large stake in demonstrating the new strategy, using Vietnam as a test case. Success in Vietnam would be regarded by Peiping as vindication for China's views in the worldwide ideological struggle.

America's History of Defending Freedom in Southeast Asia

Taking into account the relationship of Vietnam to Indochina—and of both to Southeast Asia, the Far East, and the free world as a whole—five United States Presidents have acted to preserve free world strategic interests in the area.

President [Franklin] Roosevelt opposed Japanese penetration in Indochina; President [Harry S.] Truman resisted Communist aggression in Korea; President [Dwight] Eisenhower backed Diem's efforts to save South Vietnam and undertook to defend Taiwan; President Kennedy stepped up our counterinsurgency effort in Vietnam; and President Johnson, in addition to reaffirming last week [in March 1964] that the United States will furnish assistance and support to South Vietnam for as long as it is required to bring Communist aggression and terrorism under control, has approved the program that I shall describe in a few minutes.

The United States' role in South Vietnam, then, is: First, to answer the call of the South Vietnamese, a member of our free world family, to help them save their country for themselves; second, to help prevent the strategic danger which would exist if Communism absorbed Southeast Asia's people and resources; and third, to prove in the Vietnamese test case that the free world can cope with Communist "wars of liberation" as we have coped with aggression at other levels. . . .

In our concern over the seriousness of the Vietcong insurgency, we sometimes overlook the fact that a favorable comparison still exists between progress in the south—notwithstanding nearly 15 years of bitter warfare—and the relative stagnation in North Vietnam. In short, the situation in South Vietnam has unquestionably worsened, at least since last fall [1963].

The picture is admittedly not an easy one to evaluate and, given the kind of terrain and the kind of war, information is not always available or reliable. The areas under Communist control vary from daytime to nighttime, from one week to another, according to seasonal and weather factors. And, of course, in various areas the degree and importance of control differ.

> Clearly, the disciplined leadership, direction, and support from North Vietnam is a critical factor in the strength of the Vietcong movement.

Although we estimate that in South Vietnam's 14 million population there are only 20,000 to 25,000 "hard core" Vietcong guerrillas, they have been able to recruit from among the South Vietnamese an irregular force of from 60,000 to 80,000—mainly by coercion and "bandwagon" effect, but also by promising material and political rewards.

The loyalties of the hard core have been cemented by years of fighting, first against the Japanese, then against the French, and, since 1954, against the fledgling Government of South Vietnam.

The young men joining them have been attracted by the excitement of the guerrilla life and then held by bonds of loyalty to their new comrades-in-arms, in a nation where loyalty is only beginning to extend beyond the family or the clan. These loyalties are reinforced both by systematic indoctrination and by the example of what happens to informers and deserters.

Clearly, the disciplined leadership, direction, and support from North Vietnam is a critical factor in the strength of the Vietcong movement. But the large indigenous support that the Vietcong receives means that solutions must be as political and economic as military. Indeed, there can be no such thing as a purely "military" solution of the war in South Vietnam.

Faith in a Strong South Vietnam

The people of South Vietnam prefer independence and freedom. But they will not exercise their choice for freedom and commit themselves to it in the face of the high personal risk of Communist retaliation—a kidnapped son, a burned home, a ravaged crop—unless they can have confidence in the ultimate outcome.

Much therefore depends on the new Government under General [Nguyen] Khanh [one of the military leaders who deposed Ngo Dinh Diem], for which we have high hopes.

Today the Government of General Khanh is vigorously rebuilding the machinery of administration and reshaping plans to carry the war to the Vietcong. He is an able and energetic leader. He has demonstrated his grasp of the basic elements—political, economic, and psychological, as well as military—required to defeat the Vietcong. He is planning a program of economic and social advances for the welfare of his people.

He has brought into support of the Government representatives of key groups previously excluded. He and his colleagues have developed plans for systematic liberation of areas now submissive to Vietcong duress and for mobilization of all available Vietnamese resources in the defense of the homeland.

At the same time, General Khanh has understood the need to improve South Vietnam's relations with its neighbors, Cambodia and Laos; he has taken steps towards conciliation; and he has been quick and forthright in expressing his Government's regret over the recent Vietnamese violation of Cambodia's borders.

> So far as South Vietnam is concerned, we have learned from the past that the Communists rarely honor the kind of treaty that runs counter to their compulsion to expand.

In short, he demonstrated the energy, comprehension, and decision required by the difficult circumstances that he faces.

America's Commitment Reaffirmed

Before describing the means by which we hope to assist the South Vietnamese to succeed in their undertaking, let me point out the options that President Johnson had before him when he received General [Maxwell] Taylor's and my report last week [in March 1964].

Some critics of our present policy have suggested one option—that we simply withdraw. This the United States totally rejects for reasons I have stated.

Other critics have called for a second and similar option—a "neutralization" of Vietnam. This, however, is the game of "What's mine is mine and what's yours is negotiable." No one seriously believes the Communists would agree to "neutralization" of North Vietnam.

And, so far as South Vietnam is concerned, we have learned from the past that the Communists rarely honor the kind of treaty that runs counter to their compulsion to expand.

Under the shadow of Communist power, "neutralization" would in reality be an interim device to permit Communist consolidation and eventual takeover. When

General Taylor and I were in Hue, at the north end of South Vietnam, two weeks ago, several Vietnamese students carried posters which showed their recognition of the reality of "neutralization." The signs read: "Neutralize today, Communize tomorrow."

"Neutralization" of South Vietnam, which is today under unprovoked subversive attack, would not be in any sense an achievement of the objectives I have outlined. As we tried to convey in Laos, we have no objection in principle to neutrality in the sense of nonalignment. But even there we are learning lessons.

Communist abuse of the Geneva accords, by treating the Laos corridor as a sanctuary for infiltration, constantly threatens the precarious neutrality. "Neutralization of South Vietnam"—an ambiguous phrase at best—was therefore rejected.

The third option before the President was initiation of military actions outside South Vietnam, particularly against North Vietnam, in order to supplement the counterinsurgency program in South Vietnam.

This course of action—its implications and ways of carrying it out—has been carefully studied.

Whatever ultimate course of action may be forced upon us by the other side, it is clear that actions under this option would be only a supplement to, not a substitute for, progress within South Vietnam's own borders.

The fourth course of action was to concentrate on helping the South Vietnamese with the battle in their own country. This, all agree, is essential no matter what else is done.

The President therefore approved the 12 recommendations that General Taylor and I made relating to this option.

We have reaffirmed United States support for South Vietnam's Government and pledged economic assistance and military training and logistical support for as long as it takes to bring the insurgency under control.

We will support the Government of South Vietnam in carrying out its anti-insurgency plan. Under that plan, Prime Minister Khanh intends to implement a national mobilization program to mobilize all national resources in the struggle.

This means improving the quality of the strategic hamlets, building them systematically outward from secure areas, and correcting previous overextension.

The security forces of Vietnam will be increased by at least 50,000 men. They will be consolidated, and their effectiveness and conditions of service will be improved. They will press the campaign with increased intensity. We will provide required additional material.

This will include strengthening of the Vietnamese Air Force with better aircraft and improving the mobility of the ground forces.

Political and Economic Aid to Buttress Military Strength

A broad national program is to be carried out, giving top priority to rural needs. The program includes land reform, loans to tenant farmers, health and welfare measures, economic development, and improved status for ethnic minorities and paramilitary troops.

A civil administrative corps will be established to bring better public services to the people. This will include teachers, health technicians, agricultural workers, and other technicians.

> We have learned that 'peace at any price' is not practical in the long run, and that the cost of defending freedom must be borne if we are to have it at all.

The initial goal during 1964 will be at least 7,500 additional persons; ultimately there will be at least 40,000 men for more than 8,000 hamlets, in 2,500 villages and 43 provinces.

Farm productivity will be increased through doubled use of fertilizers to provide immediate and direct benefits to peasants in secure areas and to increase both their earnings and the nation's export earnings.

We have learned that in Vietnam, political and economic progress are the sine qua non of military success, and that military security is equally a prerequisite of internal progress. Our future joint efforts with the Vietnamese are going to apply these lessons.

To conclude: let me reiterate that our goal is peace and stability, both in Vietnam and Southeast Asia. But we have learned that "peace at any price" is not practical in the long run, and that the cost of defending freedom must be borne if we are to have it at all.

The road ahead in Vietnam is going to be long, difficult, and frustrating. It will take work, courage, imagination, and—perhaps more than anything else—patience to bear the burden of what President Kennedy called a "long twilight struggle."

In Vietnam, it has not been finished in the first hundred days of President Johnson's Administration, and it may not be finished in the first 1,000 days; but, in cooperation with General Khanh's Government, we have made a beginning.

When the day comes that we can safely withdraw, we expect to leave an independent and stable South Vietnam, rich with resources and bright with prospects for contributing to the peace and prosperity of Southeast Asia and of the world.

The People of the United States Become Disenchanted with the War

Saturday Evening Post

The following viewpoint is a 1967 editorial from the *Saturday Evening Post*, a venerable news and lifestyle magazine that began its publication history in 1728. In the editorial, the *Post* comments on the declining public approval ratings for President Lyndon Johnson chiefly because of his escalation of the Vietnam War. According to the editor, the public is tired of a war that has seen little progress in securing South Vietnam's freedom and has already claimed more than 100,000 American lives. Though the *Post* notes that President Johnson still has his supporters, it reports that many in the Congress believe the war is neither justified nor worth the costs.

SOURCE. *Saturday Evening Post*, v. 240, November 18, 1967. Copyright © 1967 Saturday Evening Post Society. Reproduced by permission.

It is a perilous thing to try to estimate what the American people think about anything at any given time, but there appears to be a definite change in popular feelings about the war in Vietnam. A year or two ago [1965–1966], anybody who opposed the war got a distinct feeling of loneliness, and the general view seemed to be that, regardless of whether the war was justified or not, we all had to fall in behind the leadership of the President [Lyndon Johnson]. As recently as last winter, when this magazine criticized the bombing of North Vietnam, that issue of the *Post* was read aloud before a Senate committee and excoriated as an example of wrongheadedness.

Congressmen Turn Against the Bombing of the North

In recent months the sounds in the Senate have been rather different, and the most notable denunciations of the war have come not from liberal Democrats but from moderate Republicans. There was mild-mannered Sen. Clifford Case [R-NJ] blaming the President for a "highly irresponsible" escalation of the fighting. Sen. Thruston Morton [R-KY], former G.O.P chairman, went even further. "President Johnson was brainwashed. . . . He has been mistakenly committed to a military solution in Vietnam for the past five years." Sen. John Sherman Cooper [R-KY] added: "There is little hope for negotiations and for a just settlement of the war in Vietnam until the United States takes this first step—the cessation of its bombing of North Vietnam."

> According to a recent Gallup poll . . . 57 percent of the people questioned disapproved of the President's handling of the war, compared to only 28 percent who approved.

The President's Opinion Poll Results Drop

Politicians do not speak in a vacuum. To a certain extent they reflect the opinions of the voters they represent,

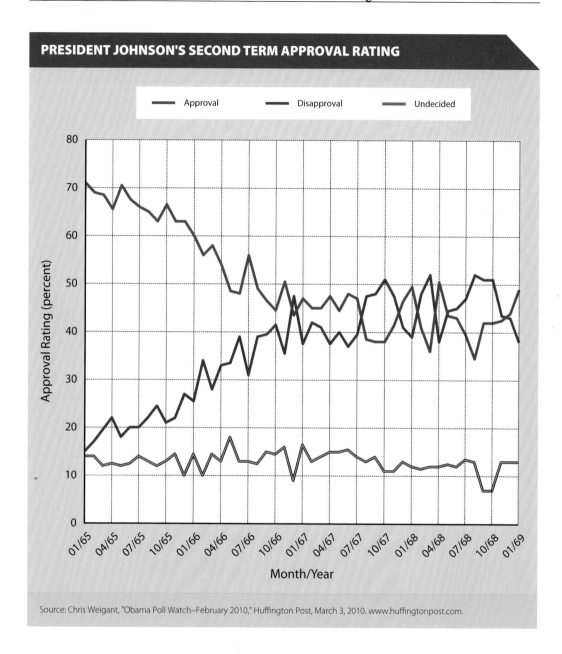

PRESIDENT JOHNSON'S SECOND TERM APPROVAL RATING

Source: Chris Weigant, "Obama Poll Watch–February 2010," Huffington Post, March 3, 2010. www.huffingtonpost.com.

and those voters no longer seem content to follow the President's course. According to a recent Gallup poll— and a Harris poll showed similar results—57 percent of the people questioned disapproved of the President's

Demonstrators in Berkeley, California, reflected growing public sentiment, which began to turn against the war in Vietnam as casualties mounted. (**AP Images.**)

handling of the war, compared to only 28 percent who approved. This was the highest rate of disapproval ever recorded in the poll, and a phenomenal rate for any democratic society engaged in a major military conflict. Some of those who disapprove of President Johnson's policy are, of course, the "superhawks," who demand unlimited military force to "get it over with." But of those who disapproved, the "superhawks" accounted for only 37 percent, while 18 percent thought the United States ought to scale down the fighting.

There are perfectly good reasons for the increasing disenchantment with this war. For one thing, the simple passage of time tends to sour the popular appetite for fighting. More American troops, more bombing, new plans for "pacification"—all these things were supposed to produce results, but the results are hard to find. On the contrary, the South Vietnamese army seems to fight less today than it did a year ago, while the Communists fight harder. Politically, too, our South Vietnamese military protégés have shown themselves unable to govern the country and unable to evolve toward democratic rule. And for Americans, the only consequence of escalation is that the price we must pay gets higher and higher. While major domestic problems go unattended, the President demands higher taxes to pay for the war. And from the battlefield, the bodies come home in ever-increasing numbers. The death toll so far this year is higher than during the previous five years combined, and the total casualty figure has already climbed to more than 100,000. In a few months, Vietnam will pass Korea as the fourth-bloodiest war in our history.

The President's Defenders

For the defense, Washington's tired warriors provide their tired arguments. Speaking on behalf of President Johnson, Republican Senate leader Everett Dirksen [IL] asked: "Have you heard the British demean their king and queen? . . . It don't sound good, and it don't look good. The president is not our ruler, but you do not demean him in the eyes of people abroad." And in an increasingly extravagant speech, Dirksen went on to declare: "Let me say that I was not made a senator to preside over the liquidation of the holy fabric of freedom." Somewhat less rhetorically,

> It has never been clear exactly who committed the United States to a major land war in Southeast Asia, nor how, or why, or to whom the commitment was made.

Secretary of State Dean Rusk's Support for the Vietnam War

As U.S. secretary of state from 1961 to 1969, Dean Rusk was one of America's major Vietnam War policy makers. . . .

Rusk viewed the Vietnam War as an important test of America's determination to contain communism and maintain its position as the world's leading democracy. In fact, he warned that if the United States broke its commitment to defend South Vietnam from its Communist neighbors, China or Russia might invade other countries in the belief that America would not intervene. He thought that such an invasion might then trigger a nuclear war between the United States and either China or Russia.

This belief led Rusk to support more aggressive U.S. military policies toward Vietnam in the mid-1960s, when it appeared that the South was in danger of falling to the Communists. He abandoned his previous opposition to using American troops in the conflict and joined U.S. secretary of defense Robert McNamara in advocating a military strategy of gradual escalation toward North Vietnam and the Viet Cong. Persuaded by this advice, President Lyndon Johnson committed large numbers of American troops to the South's defense. He also launched bombing campaigns and other new operations against the North. Before long, the United States had assumed primary responsibility for defeating the Communists in Vietnam.

SOURCE. *"Dean Rusk,"* Vietnam War Reference Library. *Vol. 2: Biographies. Detroit: UXL, 2001.*

but no less passionately, Secretary of State Dean Rusk insisted that the war represented an honoring of "commitments." Though it has never been clear exactly who committed the United States to a major land war in Southeast Asia, nor how, or why, or to whom the commitment was made, Secretary Rusk declared: "Let me say, as solemnly as I can, that those who would place in question the credibility of the pledged word of the United States under our mutual security treaties would subject this nation to mortal danger." As for stopping the bombing of North Vietnam, Rusk's answer was scornful: "Let's not be children."

Secretary Rusk is responsible only to President Johnson, of course, and President Johnson seems to be responsible to nobody. Back in the days when his critics were in the minority, the President used to flourish polls to show that the people loved him. Now that the polls show a majority opposed to him, the President talks mournfully about the need for noble leaders to carry out unpopular policies for the greater good of the nation. There have been times when this was true. But there have also been times when leaders have made terrible mistakes and refused, through pride and stubbornness, to correct them. The war in Vietnam is Johnson's mistake, and, through the power of his office, he has made it a national mistake. More and more Americans have come to see this, and that is the message of the polls that the President now ignores.

America Will Have a Just Peace in Vietnam

Richard Nixon

By 1969, when President Richard Nixon inherited the Vietnam War from his predecessor, Lyndon Johnson, the U.S. home front was plagued with doubt over the progress of the war. Numerous demonstrations filled city streets calling for a withdrawal of U.S. soldiers from Vietnam. Nixon believed that most Americans, however, believed in the justness of the U.S. mission in Vietnam and did not wish to face an ignominious defeat. According to him, this "silent majority"—so named because their voices were not heard above the clamoring of the antiwar factions that garnered the most news coverage—was hopeful that the United States could still "win the peace" even if it lost the war. In the following viewpoint, Nixon reaches out to the silent majority in a televised address to the nation, explaining that his administration has tried to negotiate for peace with North Vietnam but has encountered a regime that is unwilling to compromise. Given the lack of momentum at the peace table, Nixon asserts that he plans to slowly "Vietnamize" the war—that is, to force the South

SOURCE. Richard Nixon, Address to the Nation on the War in Vietnam, November 3, 1969.

Vietnamese to do the bulk of the fighting for their own freedom and begin to bring U.S. troops home. Nixon assures the public and foreign powers that the United States will not abandon South Vietnam, but he makes clear that the United States cannot be the primary fighting force in nations where native armies are capable of providing defense.

Good evening, my fellow Americans:
Tonight I want to talk to you on a subject of deep concern to all Americans and to many people in all parts of the world—the war in Vietnam.

I believe that one of the reasons for the deep division about Vietnam is that many Americans have lost confidence in what their Government has told them about our policy. The American people cannot and should not be asked to support a policy which involves the overriding issues of war and peace unless they know the truth about that policy.

Tonight, therefore, I would like to answer some of the questions that I know are on the minds of many of you listening to me.

How and why did America get involved in Vietnam in the first place?

How has this administration changed the policy of the previous administration?

What has really happened in the negotiations in Paris and on the battlefront in Vietnam?

What choices do we have if we are to end the war?

What are the prospects for peace?

The Situation Nixon Inherited

Now, let me begin by describing the situation I found when I was inaugurated on January 20 [1969].

- The war had been going on for 4 years.
- 31,000 Americans had been killed in action.

- The training program for the South Vietnamese was behind schedule.

- 540,000 Americans were in Vietnam with no plans to reduce the number.

- No progress had been made at the negotiations in Paris and the United States had not put forth a comprehensive peace proposal.

- The war was causing deep division at home and criticism from many of our friends as well as our enemies abroad.

In view of these circumstances there were some who urged that I end the war at once by ordering the immediate withdrawal of all American forces.

From a political standpoint this would have been a popular and easy course to follow. After all, we became involved in the war while my predecessor was in office. I could blame the defeat which would be the result of my action on him and come out as the Peacemaker. Some put it to me quite bluntly: This was the only way to avoid allowing [President Lyndon] Johnson's war to become Nixon's war.

> The great question is: How can we win America's peace?

But I had a greater obligation than to think only of the years of my administration and of the next election. I had to think of the effect of my decision on the next generation and on the future of peace and freedom in America and in the world.

Winning the Peace

Let us all understand that the question before us is not whether some Americans are for peace and some Americans are against peace. The question at issue is not whether Johnson's war becomes Nixon's war.

The great question is: How can we win America's peace?

Well, let us turn now to the fundamental issue. Why and how did the United States become involved in Vietnam in the first place?

Fifteen years ago [in 1954], North Vietnam, with the logistical support of Communist China and the Soviet Union, launched a campaign to impose a Communist government on South Vietnam by instigating and supporting a revolution.

In response to the request of the Government of South Vietnam, President [Dwight] Eisenhower sent economic aid and military equipment to assist the people of South Vietnam in their efforts to prevent a Communist takeover. Seven years ago, President [John F.] Kennedy sent 16,000 military personnel to Vietnam as combat advisers. Four years ago, President Johnson sent American combat forces to South Vietnam.

Now, many believe that President Johnson's decision to send American combat forces to South Vietnam was wrong. And many others—I among them—have been strongly critical of the way the war has been conducted.

But the question facing us today is: Now that we are in the war, what is the best way to end it?

In January I could only conclude that the precipitate withdrawal of American forces from Vietnam would be a disaster not only for South Vietnam but for the United States and for the cause of peace.

For the South Vietnamese, our precipitate withdrawal would inevitably allow the Communists to repeat the massacres which followed their takeover in the North 15 years before.

- They then murdered more than 50,000 people and hundreds of thousands more died in slave labor camps.

- We saw a prelude of what would happen in South Vietnam when the Communists entered the city of Hue last year. During their brief rule there, there was a bloody reign of terror in which 3,000 civilians were clubbed, shot to death, and buried in mass graves.

- With the sudden collapse of our support, these atrocities of Hue would become the nightmare of the entire nation and particularly for the million and a half Catholic refugees who fled to South Vietnam when the Communists took over in the North.

For the United States, this first defeat in our Nation's history would result in a collapse of confidence in American leadership, not only in Asia but throughout the world.

> A nation cannot remain great if it betrays its allies and lets down its friends.

Three American Presidents have recognized the great stakes involved in Vietnam and understood what had to be done.

In 1963, President Kennedy, with his characteristic eloquence and clarity, said: ". . . we want to see a stable government there, carrying on a struggle to maintain its national independence.

"We believe strongly in that. We are not going to withdraw from that effort. In my opinion, for us to withdraw from that effort would mean a collapse not only of South Viet-Nam, but Southeast Asia. So we are going to stay there."

President Eisenhower and President Johnson expressed the same conclusion during their terms of office.

For the future of peace, precipitate withdrawal would thus be a disaster of immense magnitude.

- A nation cannot remain great if it betrays its allies and lets down its friends.
- Our defeat and humiliation in South Vietnam without question would promote recklessness in the councils of those great powers who have not yet abandoned their goals of world conquest.

- This would spark violence wherever our commitments help maintain the peace—in the Middle East, in Berlin, eventually even in the Western Hemisphere.

Ultimately, this would cost more lives.
It would not bring peace; it would bring more war.

Opening Negotiations

For these reasons, I rejected the recommendation that I should end the war by immediately withdrawing all of our forces. I chose instead to change American policy on both the negotiating front and battlefront.

In order to end a war fought on many fronts, I initiated a pursuit for peace on many fronts.

In a television speech on May 14, in a speech before the United Nations, and on a number of other occasions, I set forth our peace proposals in great detail.

- We have offered the complete withdrawal of all outside forces within 1 year.

- We have proposed a cease-fire under international supervision.

- We have offered free elections under international supervision with the Communists participating in the organization and conduct of the elections as an organized political force. And the Saigon Government has pledged to accept the result of the elections.

We have not put forth our proposals on a take-it-or-leave-it basis. We have indicated that we are willing to discuss the proposals that have been put forth by the other side. We have declared that anything is negotiable except the right of the people of South Vietnam to determine their own future. At the Paris peace conference, [U.S.] Ambassador [Henry

> Hanoi has refused even to discuss our proposals.

Cabot] Lodge has demonstrated our flexibility and good faith in 40 public meetings.

Hanoi has refused even to discuss our proposals. They demand our unconditional acceptance of their terms, which are that we withdrew all American forces immediately and unconditionally and that we overthrow the Government of South Vietnam as we leave.

We have not limited our peace initiatives to public forums and public statements. I recognized, in January, that a long and bitter war like this usually cannot be settled in a public forum. That is why in addition to the public statements and negotiations I have explored every possible private avenue that might lead to a settlement. . . .

But the effect of all the public, private, and secret negotiations which have been undertaken since the bombing halt a year ago and since this administration came into office on January 20, can be summed up in one sentence: No progress whatever has been made except agreement on the shape of the bargaining table.

Well now, who is at fault?

It has become clear that the obstacle in negotiating an end to the war is not the President of the United States. It is not the South Vietnamese Government.

The obstacle is the other side's absolute refusal to show the least willingness to join us in seeking a just peace. And it will not do so while it is convinced that all it has to do is to wait for our next concession, and our next concession after that one, until it gets everything it wants.

There can now be no longer any question that progress in negotiation depends only on Hanoi's deciding to negotiate, to negotiate seriously.

I realize that this report on our efforts on the diplomatic front is discouraging to the American people, but the American people are entitled to know the truth—the bad news as well as the good news—where the lives of our young men are involved.

The Nixon Doctrine

Now let me turn, however, to a more encouraging report on another front.

At the time we launched our search for peace I recognized we might not succeed in bringing an end to the war through negotiation. I, therefore, put into effect another plan to bring peace—a plan which will bring the war to an end regardless of what happens on the negotiating front.

It is in line with a major shift in U.S. foreign policy which I described in my press conference at Guam on July 25. Let me briefly explain what has been described

U.S. president Richard Nixon justified the United States' continued intervention in Vietnam on the grounds of North Vietnamese atrocities in the city of Hue, seen here after the devastating Tet Offensive of 1968. (AP Images.)

as the Nixon Doctrine—a policy which not only will help end the war in Vietnam, but which is an essential element of our program to prevent future Vietnams.

We Americans are a do-it-yourself people. We are an impatient people. Instead of teaching someone else to do a job, we like to do it ourselves. And this trait has been carried over into our foreign policy.

In Korea and again in Vietnam, the United States furnished most of the money, most of the arms, and most of the men to help the people of those countries defend their freedom against Communist aggression.

Before any American troops were committed to Vietnam, a leader of another Asian country expressed this opinion to me when I was traveling in Asia as a private citizen. He said: "When you are trying to assist another nation defend its freedom, U.S. policy should be to help them fight the war but not to fight the war for them."

Well, in accordance with this wise counsel, I laid down in Guam three principles as guidelines for future American policy toward Asia:

- First, the United States will keep all of its treaty commitments.

- Second, we shall provide a shield if a nuclear power threatens the freedom of a nation allied with us or of a nation whose survival we consider vital to our security.

- Third, in cases involving other types of aggression, we shall furnish military and economic assistance when requested in accordance with our treaty commitments. But we shall look to the nation directly threatened to assume the primary responsibility of providing the manpower for its defense.

After I announced this policy, I found that the leaders of the Philippines, Thailand, Vietnam, South Korea, and other nations which might be threatened by Communist aggression, welcomed this new direction in American foreign policy.

The defense of freedom is everybody's business—not just America's business. And it is particularly the responsibility of the people whose freedom is threatened. In the previous administration, we Americanized the war in Vietnam. In this administration, we are Vietnamizing the search for peace.

> The defense of freedom is everybody's business—not just America's business.

The policy of the previous administration not only resulted in our assuming the primary responsibility for fighting the war, but even more significantly did not adequately stress the goal of strengthening the South Vietnamese so that they could defend themselves when we left.

The Vietnamization plan was launched following Secretary [of Defense Melvin R.] Laird's visit to Vietnam in March. Under the plan, I ordered first a substantial increase in the training and equipment of South Vietnamese forces.

In July, on my visit to Vietnam, I changed [overall U.S. military commander in Vietnam] General [Creighton] Abrams' orders so that they were consistent with the objectives of our new policies. Under the new orders, the primary mission of our troops is to enable the South Vietnamese forces to assume the full responsibility for the security of South Vietnam.

Our air operations have been reduced by over 20 percent.

And now we have begun to see the results of this long overdue change in American policy in Vietnam.

- After 5 years of Americans going into Vietnam, we are finally bringing American men home. By December 15, over 60,000 men will have been withdrawn from South Vietnam—including 20 percent of all of our combat forces.

- The South Vietnamese have continued to gain in strength. As a result they have been able to take over combat responsibilities from our American troops.

Two other significant developments have occurred since this administration took office.

- Enemy infiltration, infiltration which is essential if they are to launch a major attack, over the last 3 months is less than 20 percent of what it was over the same period last year.
- Most important-United States casualties have declined during the last 2 months to the lowest point in 3 years.

> As South Vietnamese forces become stronger, the rate of American withdrawal can become greater.

Let me now turn to our program for the future.

We have adopted a plan which we have worked out in cooperation with the South Vietnamese for the complete withdrawal of all U.S. combat ground forces, and their replacement by South Vietnamese forces on an orderly scheduled timetable. This withdrawal will be made from strength and not from weakness. As South Vietnamese forces become stronger, the rate of American withdrawal can become greater.

Timetable for Withdrawal

I have not and do not intend to announce the timetable for our program. And there are obvious reasons for this decision which I am sure you will understand. As I have indicated on several occasions, the rate of withdrawal will depend on developments on three fronts.

One of these is the progress which can be or might be made in the Paris [peace] talks. An announcement of a fixed timetable for our withdrawal would completely remove any incentive for the enemy to negotiate an agreement. They would simply wait until our forces had withdrawn and then move in.

The other two factors on which we will base our withdrawal decisions are the level of enemy activity and the progress of the training programs of the South Vietnamese forces. And I am glad to be able to report tonight progress on both of these fronts has been greater than we anticipated when we started the program in June for withdrawal. As a result, our timetable for withdrawal is more optimistic now than when we made our first estimates in June. Now, this clearly demonstrates why it is not wise to be frozen in on a fixed timetable.

We must retain the flexibility to base each withdrawal decision on the situation as it is at that time rather than on estimates that are no longer valid.

Along with this optimistic estimate, I must—in all candor—leave one note of caution.

If the level of enemy activity significantly increases, we might have to adjust our timetable accordingly.

However, I want the record to be completely clear on one point.

At the time of the bombing halt just a year ago, there was some confusion as to whether there was an understanding on the part of the enemy that if we stopped the bombing of North Vietnam they would stop the shelling of cities in South Vietnam. I want to be sure that there is no misunderstanding on the part of the enemy with regard to our withdrawal program.

We have noted the reduced level of infiltration, the reduction of our casualties, and are basing our withdrawal decisions partially on those factors.

If the level of infiltration or our casualties increase while we are trying to scale down the fighting, it will be the result of a conscious decision by the enemy.

Hanoi could make no greater mistake than to assume that an increase in violence will be to its advantage. If I conclude that increased enemy action jeopardizes our remaining forces in Vietnam, I shall not hesitate to take strong and effective measures to deal with that situation.

This is not a threat. This is a statement of policy, which as Commander in Chief of our Armed Forces, I am making in meeting my responsibility for the protection of American fighting men wherever they may be.

My fellow Americans, I am sure you can recognize from what I have said that we really only have two choices open to us if we want to end this war.

- I can order an immediate, precipitate withdrawal of all Americans from Vietnam without regard to the effects of that action.

- Or we can persist in our search for a just peace through a negotiated settlement if possible, or through continued implementation of our plan for Vietnamization if necessary—a plan in which we will withdraw all of our forces from Vietnam on a schedule in accordance with our program, as the South Vietnamese become strong enough to defend their own freedom.

I have chosen this second course.

It is not the easy way.

It is the right way.

It is a plan which will end the war and serve the cause of peace—not just in Vietnam but in the Pacific and in the world. . . .

There are powerful personal reasons I want to end this war. This week I will have to sign 83 letters to mothers, fathers, wives, and loved ones of men who have given their lives for America in Vietnam. It is very little satisfaction to me that this is only one-third as many letters as I signed the first week in office. There is nothing I want more than to see the day come when I do not have to write any of those letters.

- I want to end the war to save the lives of those brave young men in Vietnam.

- But I want to end it in a way which will increase the chance that their younger brothers and their sons will not have to fight in some future Vietnam someplace in the world.

- And I want to end the war for another reason. I want to end it so that the energy and dedication of you, our young people, now too often directed into bitter hatred against those responsible for the war, can be turned to the great challenges of peace, a better life for all Americans, a better life for all people on this earth.

I have chosen a plan for peace. I believe it will succeed.

If it does succeed, what the critics say now won't matter. If it does not succeed, anything I say then won't matter.

I know it may not be fashionable to speak of patriotism or national destiny these days. But I feel it is appropriate to do so on this occasion

Two hundred years ago this Nation was weak and poor. But even then, America was the hope of millions in the world. Today we have become the strongest and richest nation in the world. And the wheel of destiny has turned so that any hope the world has for the survival of peace and freedom will be determined by whether the American people have the moral stamina and the courage to meet the challenge of free world leadership.

Let historians not record that when America was the most powerful nation in the world we passed on the other side of the road and allowed the last hopes for peace and freedom of millions of people to be suffocated by the forces of totalitarianism.

And so tonight—to you, the great silent majority of my fellow Americans—I ask for your support.

> North Vietnam cannot defeat or humiliate the United States. Only Americans can do that.

I pledged in my campaign for the Presidency to end the war in a way that we could win the peace. I have initiated a plan of action which will enable me to keep that pledge.

The more support I can have from the American people, the sooner that pledge can be redeemed; for the more divided we are at home, the less likey the enemy is to negotiate at Paris.

Let us be united for peace. Let us also be united against defeat. Because let us understand: North Vietnam cannot defeat or humiliate the United States. Only Americans can do that.

Fifty years ago, in this room and at this very desk, President Woodrow Wilson spoke words which caught the imagination of a war-weary world. He said: "This is the war to end war." His dream for peace after World War I was shattered on the hard realities of great power politics and Woodrow Wilson died a broken man.

Tonight I do not tell you that the war in Vietnam is the war to end wars. But I do say this: I have initiated a plan which will end this war in a way that will bring us closer to that great goal to which Woodrow Wilson and every American President in our history has been dedicated—the goal of a just and lasting peace.

As President I hold the responsibility for choosing the best path to that goal and then leading the Nation along it.

I pledge to you tonight that I shall meet this responsibility with all of the strength and wisdom I can command in accordance with your hopes, mindful of your concerns, sustained by your prayers.

Thank you and good night.

The North Vietnamese Claim Victory in Saigon

Van Tien Dung

From April 26 to April 30, 1975, the North Vietnamese People's Army of Vietnam (PAVN) carried out the Ho Chi Minh Campaign to overtake the South Vietnamese capital of Saigon and unify the country after more than twenty years of division. In the viewpoint that follows, the chief of staff of the PAVN recalls the events of this campaign and the final retreat of the U.S. military out of the South. He tells of the joy felt throughout the country as evidenced by the assistance provided to PAVN soldiers by peasants in the South as the army advanced toward the South Vietnamese capital. Dung attributes the North's victory to the Communist party's program of propaganda, education, and organization, which unified both the soldiers and the people behind Ho Chi Minh and the liberation and unification efforts. Van Tien Dung was born a peasant, but rose through the ranks of the PAVN, serving as chief of staff from 1954 to 1974 and commander in chief from 1974 to 1980.

SOURCE. Van Tien Dung, *Our Great Spring Victory: An Account of the Liberation of South Vietnam.* Translated by John Spragens, Jr. Monthly Review Books, 1977. Copyright © 1977 verso. Republished with permission of Monthly Review Foundation, conveyed through Copyright Clearance Center, Inc.

As it unfolds, our history occasionally repeats itself. As with our forefathers in those nights before final strategic general offensives against foreign invaders, our fighters on the Saigon front on the night of April 29 [1975] and early the next morning were restless, determined to win lightning victory. In these sacred hours, in this final day of the period determined by the Political Bureau for the Liberation of Saigon, the fighters wrote on their helmets, on their sleeves, on their gun slings the immortal proclamation of [North Vietnam's] President Ho Chi Minh:

Forward! Total victory is ours!

The Americans Retreat

In those final days of April, our military delegation witnessed the end-of-the-line haste and bewilderment of the Americans and their protégés. In the past, our delegation's headquarters had often been blockaded and provoked, and had suffered many difficulties, like having electricity and water cut off, or not being allowed contact with the outside. But during these days, this was the place the enemy came most often seeking favors. [U.S.] Ambassador [Graham] Martin asked to meet a representative of our delegation. We declined. And the quisling [traitor or puppet] administration asked our delegation for permission to appoint a person to fly to Hanoi [the capital of North Vietnam] to negotiate a ceasefire. We turned that down, too.

[Vietnamese Foreign Minister] Nguyen Duy Trinh sent a telegram to inform us that the Americans' and puppets' cunning diplomatic plans coming one on top of the other, coupled with threatening hints to us, were aimed at blocking our troops' general offensive on Saigon, and showed all the more that we must fight more urgently, attack more quickly, and make the best use of each hour, each minute for total victory.

When it was almost light, the American news services reported that Martin had cleared out of Saigon in a helicopter. This viceregal mandarin, the final American plenipotentiary [diplomatic agent] in South Vietnam, beat a most hasty and pitiful retreat. As it happened, up until the day he left Saigon, Martin still felt certain that the quisling administration could be preserved, and that a ceasefire could be arranged, so he was halfhearted about the evacuation, waiting and watching. He went all the way out to Tan Son Nhat airfield to observe the situation. Our barrage of bombs and our fierce shelling had nearly paralyzed this vital airfield, and the fixed-wing aircraft they had intended to use for their evacuation could no longer operate. The encirclement of Saigon was growing tighter by the day. The Duong Van Minh card[1] which they had played far too late proved useless. When Martin reported this to Washington, President [Gerald] Ford issued orders to begin a helicopter evacuation. Coming in waves for eighteen hours straight, they carried more than 1,000 Americans and over 5,000 of their Vietnamese retainers, along with their families, out of the South. Ford also ordered Martin to evacuate immediately "without a minute's delay."

> Coming in waves for eighteen hours straight, [helicopters] carried more than 1,000 Americans and over 5,000 of their Vietnamese retainers, along with their families, out of the South.

The North Vietnamese Troops Close in on Saigon

The American evacuation was carried out from the tops of thirteen tall buildings chosen as landing pads for their helicopters. The number of these landing pads shrank gradually as tongues of fire from our advancing troops came closer. At the American embassy, the boarding point for the evacuation copters was a scene of monumental confusion, with the Americans, flunkies

The Paris Peace Accords

After nearly five years of negotiations between the United States and North Vietnam, the Paris peace accords were signed on 25 January 1973. Essentially the same agreement had been reached three months earlier, but intransigence over details and South Vietnam's refusal to cooperate delayed the treaty. In December 1972, President [Richard] Nixon ordered the heaviest bombing of the war to intimidate North Vietnam and to reassure South Vietnam. Another week of talks between [Secretary of State] Henry Kissinger and [chief spokesperson of the North Vietnam peace delegation] Le Duc Tho finally resulted in an agreement in which both sides accepted a cease-fire under international supervision and obtained their key demands. North Vietnam retained control over large areas of the south, left its troops in place there, and continued to receive Soviet and Chinese aid. The United States gained a "decent interval" to withdraw its troops and obtain the release of prisoners of war. South Vietnam received promises from North Vietnam not to invade and U.S. promises of reintervention if the agreement broke down. "We have finally achieved peace with honor," Nixon told the American public. Within sixty days the last U.S. troops departed, and military aid to South Vietnam was cut off entirely. . . .

North Vietnam vowed to unify the country by force if necessary, and Nixon promised to resume bombing and military aid if South Vietnam were attacked. But Congress refused to send more aid or permit bombing, and the Watergate scandal forced Nixon from office. After two years, North Vietnam broke the Paris accords with a massive conventional invasion that ended the war in 1975.

SOURCE. *Glen Gendeel, "Paris Accords,"* Encyclopedia of the Vietnam War. *Ed. Stanley I. Kutler. New York: Charles Scribner's Sons, 1996.*

fighting their way in, smashing doors, climbing walls, climbing each other's backs, tussling, brawling, and trampling each other as they sought to flee. It reached the point where Martin, who wanted to return to his own house for his suitcase before he fled, had to take a back street, using the rear gate of the embassy. When "Code 2," Martin's code name, and "Lady 09," the name of the helicopter carrying him, left the embassy for the East Sea, it signaled the shameful defeat of U.S. imperialism after thirty years of intervention and military adventures in Vietnam. At the height of their invasion of Vietnam, the U.S. had used 60 percent of their total infantry, 58 percent of their marines, 32 percent of their tactical air force, 50 percent of their strategic air force, fifteen of their eighteen aircraft carriers, 800,000 American troops (counting those stationed in satellite countries who were taking part in the Vietnam war), and more than 1 million Saigon troops. They mobilized as many as 6 million American soldiers in rotation, dropped over 10 million tons of bombs, and spent over $300 billion, but in the end the U.S. ambassador had to crawl up to the helicopter pad looking for a way to flee. Today, looking back on the gigantic force the enemy had mobilized, recalling the malicious designs they admitted, and thinking about the extreme difficulties and complexities which our revolutionary sampan had had to pass through, we were all the more aware how immeasurably great this campaign to liberate Saigon and liberate the South was. . . .

Solidarity Among the North Vietnamese Fighters

The most extraordinary thing about this historic campaign was what had sprouted in the souls of our cadres and fighters. Why were our soldiers so heroic and determined during this campaign? What had given all of them this clear understanding of the great resolution of the party and of the nation, this clear understanding of our immeasurably precious opportunity, and this clear understanding of our unprecedented manner of fighting? What had made them so extraordinarily courageous and intense, so outstanding in their political acumen in this final phase of the war?

The will and competence of our soldiers were not achieved in a day, but were the result of a continuous process of carrying out the party's ideological and organizational work in the armed forces. And throughout our thirty years of struggle, there had been no campaign in which Uncle Ho had not gone into the operation with our soldiers. Going out to battle this time, our whole army had been given singular, unprecedented strength because this strategically decisive battle bore his name: Ho Chi Minh, for every one of our cadres and fighters, was faith, strength, and life. Among the myriad troops in all the advancing wings, every one of our fighters carried toward Ho Chi Minh City the hopes of the nation and a love for our land. Today each fighter could see with his own eyes the resiliency which the Fatherland had built up during these many years, and given his own resiliency there was nothing, no enemy scheme that could stop him.

> Wherever [the People's Army of Vietnam] went, a forest of revolutionary flags appeared, and people poured out to cheer them.

The Support of the Masses

Our troops advanced rapidly to the five primary objectives, and then spread out from there. Wherever they went, a forest of revolutionary flags appeared, and people poured out to cheer them, turning the streets of Saigon into a giant festival. From the Binh Phoc bridge to Quan Tre, people carrying flags, beating drums and hollow wooden fish, and calling through megaphones, chased down the enemy, disarmed enemy soldiers, neutralized traitors and spies, and guided our soldiers. In Hoc Mon on Route 1, the people all came out into the road to greet the soldiers, guide them, and point out the hiding places of enemy thugs. Everywhere people used megaphones to call on Saigon soldiers to take off their uniforms and lay down their guns. The people of the city, especially the

Refugees attempt to scale the wall of the U.S. embassy on April 29, 1975, when Saigon fell to the North Vietnamese invasion, ending the Vietnam War. (AP Images/Neil Ulevich.)

workers, protected factories and warehouses and turned them over to our soldiers. In all the districts bordering the city—Binh Hoa, Thanh My Tay, Phu Nhuan, Go Vap, and Thu Duc—members of the revolutionary infrastructure and other people distributed leaflets, raised flags, called on enemy soldiers to drop their guns, and supplied and guided our soldiers. Before this great army entered the city, the great cause of our nation and the policies of our revolution had entered the hearts of the people.

We were very pleased to hear that the people of the city rose up when the military attacks, going one step ahead, had given them the leverage. The masses had entered this decisive battle at just the right time, not too early, but not too late. The patriotic actions of the people created a revolutionary atmosphere of vast strength on all the city's streets. This was the most precious aspect of the mass movement in Saigon-Gia Dinh [the capital city and a neighboring province], the result of many years of propaganda, education, organizing, and training by the municipal party branch. When the opportune moment arrived, those political troops had risen up with a vanguard spirit, and advanced in giant strides along with our powerful main-force divisions, resolutely, intelligently, and courageously. The people of the city not only carried flags and food and drink for the troops, but helped disperse large numbers of enemy soldiers, forced many to surrender, chased and captured many of those who were hiding out, and preserved order and security in the streets. And we will never forget the widespread and moving images of thousands, of tens of thousands of people enthusiastically giving directions to our soldiers and guiding them as they entered the city, and helping all the wings of troops strike quickly and unexpectedly at enemy positions. Those nameless heroes of Saigon-Gia Dinh brought into the general offensive the fresh and beautiful features of people's war.

The Revolutionary Flag Flies from "Independence Palace"

As we looked at the combat operations map, the five wings of our troops seemed like five lotuses blossoming out from our five major objectives. The First Army Corps had captured Saigon's General Staff headquarters and the command compounds of all the enemy armed services. When the Third Army Corps captured Tan Son Nhat, they met one wing of troops already encamped there—our military delegation at Camp Davis; it was an amazing and moving meeting. The Fourth Army Corps captured Saigon's Ministry of Defense, the Bach Dang port, and the radio station. The 232nd force took the Special Capital Zone headquarters and the Directorate-General of Police. The Second Army Corps seized "Independence Palace," the place where the quisling leaders, those hirelings of the United States, had sold our independence, traded in human blood, and carried on their smuggling. Our soldiers immediately rushed upstairs to the place where the quisling cabinet was meeting, and arrested the whole central leadership of the Saigon administration, including their president, right on the spot. Our soldiers' vigorous actions and firm declarations revealed the spirit of a victorious army. By 11:30 A.M. on April 30 the revolutionary flag flew from "Independence Palace"; this became the meeting point for all the wings of liberating troops.

At the front headquarters, we turned on our radios to listen. The voice of the quisling president called on his troops to put down their weapons and surrender unconditionally to our troops. Saigon was completely liberated! Total victory! We were completely victorious! All of us at headquarters jumped up and shouted, embraced and carried each other around on our shoulders. The sound of applause, laughter, and happy, noisy, chattering speech was as festive as if spring had just burst upon us. It was an indescribably joyous scene. Le Duc Tho and Pham Hung embraced me and all the cadres and fighters present. We were all so happy we were choked with emotion. I lit a cigarette and smoked. Dinh Duc Thien, his eyes somewhat red, said, "Now if these eyes close, my heart will be at rest." This historic and sacred, intoxicating and completely satisfying moment was one that comes once in a generation, once in many generations. Our generation had known many victorious mornings, but there had been no morning so fresh and beautiful, so radiant,

> The entire land danced to celebrate the day of true peace after thirty years of war, the day our division had been wiped out and the suffering of separation ended.

so clear and cool, so sweet-scented as this morning of total victory, a morning which made babes older than their years and made old men young again. . . .

Vietnam Is Reunited

All of Hanoi poured out into the streets lighting firecrackers, throwing flowers, waving flags. Hanoi, the capital of the whole country, heroic Hanoi, home of Uncle Ho and our party, had accomplished this victory, along with the entire country. Forests of people, seas of people, flooded the streets singing. The whole land turned out in the streets to breathe deep the air of this perfectly happy day. The entire land danced to celebrate the day of true peace after thirty years of war, the day our division had been wiped out and the suffering of separation ended.

All the people, except for the clique of traitors, were overflowing with pride and excitement, and raised high the songs of victory. Their faces had never been so beautiful as today. Our heroic people were worthy of this great exploit, and this historic victory had itself depended heavily on their immense labors and great sacrifices. From now on, our land was unified in one span, our network of mountains and rivers again one, peace truly unambiguous, independence truly complete. Families would be brought together, and the nation, too, would be reunited.

Note

1. Duong Van Minh was named president of South Vietnam on April 28, 1975, and sought to negotiate an end to the conflict.

CHAPTER 2

Controversies Surrounding the Vietnam War

The United States Has a Duty to Defend Freedom in Vietnam

Lyndon B. Johnson

Photo on previous page: U.S. military planes spray Agent Orange over South Vietnamese foliage, turning formerly lush green fields into dead and infertile land. (Dick Swanson/ Contributor/Time & Life Pictures/Getty Images.)

In the following viewpoint, President Lyndon B. Johnson addresses the faculty and student body of Johns Hopkins University in Maryland, explaining why the United States is fighting in Vietnam. He states that the United States is not fighting to secure territory or other gains in Southeast Asia, but to fulfill its pledge to defend freedom in any nation struggling against tyranny. Johnson believes that from the turmoil of war in the world will come a new world order in which countries will work cooperatively to meet the basic needs of all people. The president contends that all Americans should work toward that goal in war and in peace. Johnson served as the thirty-sixth president of the United States. His administration oversaw the first deployment of combat troops to Vietnam and the most dramatic escalation of the conflict. The growing unpopularity of the war and the declining public confidence in his leadership, however, convinced Johnson not to seek a second term in office.

SOURCE. President Lyndon B. Johnson, "Address at Johns Hopkins University: 'Peace Without Conquest,'" April 7, 1965.

Tonight Americans and Asians are dying for a world where each people may choose its own path to change.

This is the principle for which our ancestors fought in the valleys of Pennsylvania. It is the principle for which our sons fight tonight in the jungles of Viet-Nam.

Viet-Nam is far away from this quiet campus. We have no territory there, nor do we seek any. The war is dirty and brutal and difficult. And some 400 young men, born into an America that is bursting with opportunity and promise, have ended their lives on Viet-Nam's steaming soil.

Why must we take this painful road?

Why must this Nation hazard its ease, and its interest, and its power for the sake of a people so far away?

We fight because we must fight if we are to live in a world where every country can shape its own destiny. And only in such a world will our own freedom be finally secure.

This kind of world will never be built by bombs or bullets. Yet the infirmities of man are such that force must often precede reason, and the waste of war, the works of peace.

We wish that this were not so. But we must deal with the world as it is, if it is ever to be as we wish.

The Nature of the Conflict

The world as it is in Asia is not a serene or peaceful place.

The first reality is that North Viet-Nam has attacked the independent nation of South Viet-Nam. Its object is total conquest.

Of course, some of the people of South Viet-Nam are participating in attack on their own government. But trained men and supplies, orders and arms, flow in a constant stream from north to south.

This support is the heartbeat of the war.

And it is a war of unparalleled brutality. Simple farmers are the targets of assassination and kidnapping. Women and children are strangled in the night because their men are loyal to their government. And helpless villages are ravaged by sneak attacks. Large-scale raids are conducted on towns, and terror strikes in the heart of cities.

> "The confused nature of this conflict cannot mask the fact that it is the new face of an old enemy."

The confused nature of this conflict cannot mask the fact that it is the new face of an old enemy.

Over this war—and all Asia—is another reality: the deepening shadow of Communist China. The rulers in Hanoi are urged on by Peking [Beijing]. This is a regime which has destroyed freedom in Tibet, which has attacked India, and has been condemned by the United Nations for aggression in Korea. It is a nation which is helping the forces of violence in almost every continent. The contest in Viet-Nam is part of a wider pattern of aggressive purposes.

Why Are We in Viet-Nam?

Why are these realities our concern? Why are we in South Viet-Nam?

We are there because we have a promise to keep. Since 1954 every American President has offered support to the people of South Viet-Nam. We have helped to build, and we have helped to defend. Thus, over many years, we have made a national pledge to help South Viet-Nam defend its independence.

And I intend to keep that promise.

To dishonor that pledge, to abandon this small and brave nation to its enemies, and to the terror that must follow, would be an unforgivable wrong.

We are also there to strengthen world order. Around the globe, from Berlin to Thailand, are people whose well-being rests, in part, on the belief that they can count on us if they are attacked. To leave Viet-Nam to its fate would shake the confidence of all these people in the value of an American commitment and in the value of America's word. The result would be increased unrest and instability, and even wider war.

We are also there because there are great stakes in the balance. Let no one think for a moment that retreat from Viet-Nam would bring an end to conflict. The battle would be renewed in one country and then another. The central lesson of our time is that the appetite of aggression is never satisfied. To withdraw from one battlefield means only to prepare for the next. We must say in southeast Asia—as we did in Europe—in the words of the Bible: "Hitherto shalt thou come, but no further."

There are those who say that all our effort there will be futile—that China's power is such that it is bound to dominate all southeast Asia. But there is no end to that argument until all of the nations of Asia are swallowed up.

There are those who wonder why we have a responsibility there. Well, we have it there for the same reason that we have a responsibility for the defense of Europe. World War II was fought in both Europe and Asia, and when it ended we found ourselves with continued responsibility for the defense of freedom.

Our Objective in Viet-Nam

Our objective is the independence of South Viet-Nam, and its freedom from attack. We want nothing for ourselves—only that the people of South Viet-Nam be allowed to guide their own country in their own way.

We will do everything necessary to reach that objective. And we will do only what is absolutely necessary.

In recent months attacks on South Viet-Nam were stepped up. Thus, it

> " We will not be defeated. We will not grow tired. "

North Vietnamese women aim an anti-aircraft gun in a propaganda photo. U.S. president Lyndon Johnson emphasized the brutality of the North Vietnamese to make the case for continued involvement in Vietnam. (Central Press/Stringer/Hulton Archive/Getty Images.)

became necessary for us to increase our response and to make attacks by air. This is not a change of purpose. It is a change in what we believe that purpose requires.

We do this in order to slow down aggression.

We do this to increase the confidence of the brave people of South Viet-Nam who have bravely borne this brutal battle for so many years with so many casualties.

And we do this to convince the leaders of North Viet-Nam—and all who seek to share their conquest—of a very simple fact: We will not be defeated. We will not grow tired.

We will not withdraw, either openly or under the cloak of a meaningless agreement.

We know that air attacks alone will not accomplish all of these purposes. But it is our best and prayerful judgment that they are a necessary part of the surest road to peace.

We hope that peace will come swiftly. But that is in the hands of others besides ourselves. And we must be prepared for a long continued conflict. It will require patience as well as bravery, the will to endure as well as the will to resist.

I wish it were possible to convince others with words of what we now find it necessary to say with guns and planes: Armed hostility is futile. Our resources are equal to any challenge. Because we fight for values and we fight for principles, rather than territory or colonies, our patience and our determination are unending.

Once this is clear, then it should also be clear that the only path for reasonable men is the path of peaceful settlement.

Such peace demands an independent South Viet-Nam—securely guaranteed and able to shape its own relationships to all others—free from outside interference—tied to no alliance—a military base for no other country.

These are the essentials of any final settlement.

We will never be second in the search for such a peaceful settlement in Viet-Nam.

There may be many ways to this kind of peace: in discussion or negotiation with the governments concerned; in large groups or in small ones; in the reaffirmation of old agreements or their strengthening with new ones.

We have stated this position over and over again, fifty times and more, to friend and foe alike. And we remain ready, with this purpose, for unconditional discussions.

And until that bright and necessary day of peace we will try to keep conflict from spreading. We have no desire to see thousands die in battle—Asians or Americans. We have no desire to devastate that which the people of North Viet-Nam have built with toil and sacrifice. We will use our power with restraint and with all the wisdom that we can command.

But we will use it.

This war, like most wars, is filled with terrible irony. For what do the people of North Viet-Nam want? They want what their neighbors also desire: food for their hunger; health for their bodies; a chance to learn; progress for their country; and an end to the bondage of material misery. And they would find all these things far more readily in peaceful association with others than in the endless course of battle.

A Cooperative Effort for Development

These countries of southeast Asia are homes for millions of impoverished people. Each day these people rise at dawn and struggle through until the night to wrestle existence from the soil. They are often wracked by disease, plagued by hunger, and death comes at the early age of 40.

> Great social change—as we see in our own country now—does not always come without conflict.

Stability and peace do not come easily in such a land. Neither independence nor human dignity will ever be won, though, by arms alone. It also requires the work of peace. The American people have helped generously in times past in these works. Now there must be a much more massive effort to improve the life of man in that conflict-torn corner of our world.

The first step is for the countries of southeast Asia to associate themselves in a greatly expanded cooperative effort for development. We would hope that North Viet-Nam would take its place in the common effort just as soon as peaceful cooperation is possible. . . .

The Dream of World Order

This will be a disorderly planet for a long time. In Asia, as elsewhere, the forces of the modern world are shaking old ways and uprooting ancient civilizations. There will be turbulence and struggle and even violence. Great social change—as we see in our own country now—does not always come without conflict.

We must also expect that nations will on occasion be in dispute with us. It may be because we are rich, or powerful; or because we have made some mistakes; or because they honestly fear our intentions. However, no nation need ever fear that we desire their land, or to impose our will, or to dictate their institutions.

But we will always oppose the effort of one nation to conquer another nation.

We will do this because our own security is at stake.

> Man now has the knowledge—always before denied—to make this planet serve the real needs of the people who live on it.

But there is more to it than that. For our generation has a dream. It is a very old dream. But we have the power and now we have the opportunity to make that dream come true.

For centuries nations have struggled among each other. But we dream of a world where disputes are settled by law and reason. And we will try to make it so.

For most of history men have hated and killed one another in battle. But we dream of an end to war. And we will try to make it so.

For all existence most men have lived in poverty, threatened by hunger. But we dream of a world where all are fed and charged with hope. And we will help to make it so.

The ordinary men and women of North Viet-Nam and South Viet-Nam—of China and India—of Russia and America—are brave people. They are filled with the same proportions of hate and fear, of love and hope. Most of them want the same things for themselves and their families. Most of them do not want their sons to ever die in battle, or to see their homes, or the homes of others, destroyed.

Well, this can be their world yet. Man now has the knowledge—always before denied—to make this planet serve the real needs of the people who live on it.

I know this will not be easy. I know how difficult it is for reason to guide passion, and love to master hate. The complexities of this world do not bow easily to pure and consistent answers.

But the simple truths are there just the same. We must all try to follow them as best we can.

Human Achievement, Not War, Is Impressive

We often say how impressive power is. But I do not find it impressive at all. The guns and the bombs, the rockets and the warships, are all symbols of human failure. They are necessary symbols. They protect what we cherish. But they are witness to human folly.

A dam built across a great river is impressive.

In the countryside where I was born, and where I live, I have seen the night illuminated, and the kitchens warmed, and the homes heated, where once the cheerless night and the ceaseless cold held sway. And all this happened because electricity came to our area along the humming wires of the REA [Rural Electrification Act of 1936]. Electrification of the countryside—yes, that, too, is impressive.

A rich harvest in a hungry land is impressive.

The sight of healthy children in a classroom is impressive.

These—not mighty arms—are the achievements which the American Nation believes to be impressive.

And, if we are steadfast, the time may come when all other nations will also find it so.

Every night before I turn out the lights to sleep I ask myself this question:

Have I done everything that I can do to unite this country? Have I done everything I can to help unite the world, to try to bring peace and hope to all the peoples of the world? Have I done enough?

Ask yourselves that question in your homes—and in this hall tonight. Have we, each of us, all done all we could? Have we done enough?

We may well be living in the time foretold many years ago when it was said: "I call heaven and earth to record this day against you, that I have set before you life and death, blessing and cursing: therefore choose life, that both thou and thy seed may live."

This generation of the world must choose: destroy or build, kill or aid, hate or understand.

We can do all these things on a scale never dreamed of before.

Well, we will choose life. In so doing we will prevail over the enemies within man, and over the natural enemies of all mankind.

The United States Is Not Defending Freedom in Vietnam

Paul Potter

On April 17, 1965, the Students for a Democratic Society (SDS) organized a march on Washington, D.C., to protest U.S. involvement in the war in Vietnam. Around twenty-five thousand demonstrators listened as various speechmakers delivered their thoughts on the unjustness of war and the culpability of President Lyndon Johnson's administration for expanding the United States' role in Vietnam by sending in ground forces. Paul Potter, the president of the SDS, made an impassioned plea for an antiwar movement to combat what he saw as the oppressive nature of the U.S. government—an elected body that supported dictatorship abroad and silenced dissent at home. In the following viewpoint, an excerpt from his speech, Potter outlines why he believes the United States is not fighting for justice in Vietnam but is systematically destroying the livelihoods and self-determination of the Vietnamese people through

SOURCE. Paul Potter, speech delivered at the March on Washington to End the War in Vietnam, *The Port Huron Project: Reenactments of New Left Protest Speeches*. Milan: Charta, 2010. Reproduced by permission of the author's estate.

brutal military force and the support of a cruel puppet tyrant in South Vietnam.

Most of us grew up thinking that the United States was a strong but humble nation, that involved itself in world affairs only reluctantly, that respected the integrity of other nations and other systems, and that engaged in wars only as a last resort. This was a nation with no large standing army, with no design for external conquest; that sought primarily the opportunity to develop its own resources and its own mode of living. If at some point we began to hear vague and disturbing things about what this country had done in Latin America, China, Spain and other places, we somehow remained confident about the basic integrity of this nation's foreign policy. The Cold War with all of its neat categories and black-and-white descriptions did much to assure us that what we had been taught to believe was true.

The United States Is the Greatest Threat to World Peace

But in recent years, the withdrawal from the hysteria of the Cold War era and the development of a more aggressive, activist foreign policy have done much to force many of us to rethink attitudes that were deep and basic sentiments about our country. The incredible war in Vietnam has provided the razor, the terrifying sharp cutting edge that has finally severed the last vestige of illusion that morality and democracy are the guiding principles of American foreign policy. The saccharine self-righteous moralism that promises the Vietnamese a billion dollars of economic aid at the very moment we are delivering billions for economic and social destruction and political repression is rapidly losing what power it might ever have had to reassure us about the decency of our foreign policy. The further we explore the reality of what this country is doing and planning in Vietnam, the more we are driven toward the conclusion of Senator [Wayne] Morse [R-OR] that the United States may well be the greatest threat to peace in the world today. That is a terrible and bitter insight for people who grew up as we did; and our revulsion at that insight, our refusal to accept it as inevitable or necessary, is one of the reasons that so many people have come here today.

A U.S.-Backed Dictatorship in Vietnam

The president [Lyndon Johnson] says that we are defending freedom in Vietnam. Whose freedom? Not the freedom of the Vietnamese. The first act of the first dictator, [Ngo Dinh] Diem, the United States installed in Vietnam, was to systematically begin the persecution of all political opposition, non-Communist as well as Communist. The first American military supplies were not used to fight Communist insurgents; they were used to control, imprison or kill any who sought something better for Vietnam than the personal aggrandizement, political corruption and the profiteering of the Diem regime. The elite of the forces that we have trained and equipped are still used to control political unrest in Saigon and defend the latest dictator from the people.

And yet in a world where dictatorships are so commonplace and popular control of government so rare, people become callous to the misery that is implied by dictatorial power. The rationalizations that are used to defend political despotism have been drummed into us so long that we have somehow become numb to the possibility that something else might exist. And it is only the kind of terror we see now in Vietnam that awakens conscience and reminds us that there is something deep in us that cries out against dictatorial suppression.

The pattern of repression and destruction that we have developed and justified in the war is so thorough that it can only be called cultural genocide. I am not simply talking about napalm or gas or crop destruction or torture, hurled indiscriminately on women and children, insurgent and neutral, upon the first suspicion of rebel activity. That in itself is horrendous and incredible beyond belief. But it is only part of a larger pattern of destruction to the very fabric of the country. We have uprooted the people from the land and imprisoned them in concentration camps called "sunrise villages." Through conscription and direct political intervention and control, we have destroyed local customs and traditions, trampled upon those things of value which give dignity and purpose to life. What is left to the people of Vietnam after twenty years of war? What part of themselves and their own lives will those who survive be able to salvage from the wreckage of their country or build on the "peace" and "security" our Great Society offers them in reward for their allegiance? How can anyone be surprised that people who have had total war waged on themselves and their culture rebel in increasing numbers against that tyranny? What other course is available? And still our only response to rebellion is more vigorous repression, more merciless opposition to the social and cultural institutions which sustain dignity and the will to resist.

> By what weird logic can it be said that the freedom of one people can only be maintained by crushing another?

Not even the president can say that this is a war to defend the freedom of the Vietnamese people. Perhaps what the president means when he speaks of freedom is the freedom of the American people.

Silencing Dissent in America

What in fact has the war done for freedom in America? It has led to even more vigorous governmental efforts to control information, manipulate the press and pressure and persuade the public through distorted or down-right dishonest documents such as the "white paper" on Vietnam. It has led to the confiscation of films and other anti-war material and the vigorous harassment by the FBI of some of the people who have been most outspokenly active in their criticism of the war. As the war escalates and the administration seeks more actively to gain support for any initiative it may choose to take, there has been the beginnings of a war psychology unlike anything that has burdened this country since the 1950s. How much more of Mr. Johnson's freedom can we stand? How much freedom will be left in this country if there is a major war in Asia? By what weird logic can it be said that the freedom of one people can only be maintained by crushing another? . . .

The president mocks freedom if he insists that the war in Vietnam is a defense of American freedom. Perhaps the only freedom that this war protects is the freedom of the war hawks in the Pentagon and the State Department to experiment with counter-insurgency and guerilla warfare in Vietnam.

The Counter-Revolution Experiment

Vietnam, we may say, is a laboratory run by a new breed of gamesmen who approach war as a kind of rational exercise in international power politics. It is the testing ground and staging area for a new American response to the social revolution that is sweeping through the impoverished downtrodden areas of the world. It is the beginning of the American counter-revolution, and so far none of us—not the *New York Times*, nor 17 Neutral Nations, nor dozens of worried allies, nor the United States Congress have been able to interfere with the freedom of the president and the Pentagon to carry out that experiment.

Thus far the war in Vietnam has only dramatized the demand of ordinary people to have some oppor-

tunity to make their own lives, and of their unwilling-
ness, even under incredible odds, to give up the struggle
against external domination. We are
told, however, that the struggle can
be legitimately suppressed since it
might lead to the development of a
Communist system, and before that
ultimate menace all criticism is supposed to melt.

> What kind of system is it that justifies the United States or any country seizing the destinies of the Vietnamese people and using them callously for its own purpose?

This is a critical point and there
are several things that must be said
here—not by way of celebration, but
because I think they are the truth.
First, if this country were serious
about giving the people of Vietnam some alternative to a
Communist social revolution, that opportunity was sac-
rificed in 1954 when we helped to install Diem and his
repression of non-Communist movements. There is no
indication that we were serious about that goal—that we
were ever willing to contemplate the risks of allowing the
Vietnamese to choose their own destinies. Second, those
people who insist now that Vietnam can be neutralized
are for the most part looking for a sugar coating to cover
the bitter pill. We must accept the consequence that calling for an end of the war in Vietnam is in fact allowing
for the likelihood that a Vietnam without war will be
a self-styled Communist Vietnam. Third, this country
must come to understand that creation of a Communist
country in the world today is not an ultimate defeat. If
people are given the opportunity to choose their own
lives, it is likely that some of them will choose what we
have called "Communist systems." We are not powerless
in that situation. Recent years have finally and indis-
putably broken the myth that the Communist world is
monolithic and have conclusively shown that American
power can be significant in aiding countries dominated
by greater powers to become more independent and self-

determined. And yet the war that we are creating and escalating in Southeast Asia is rapidly eroding the base of independence of North Vietnam as it is forced to turn to China and the Soviet Union, involving them in the war and involving itself in the compromises that that implies. Fourth, I must say to you that I would rather see Vietnam Communist than see it under continuous subjugation of the ruin that American domination has brought.

A System of Materialism, Power, and Oppression

But the war goes on; the freedom to conduct that war depends on the dehumanization not only of Vietnamese people but of Americans as well; it depends on the construction of a system of premises and thinking that insulates the president and his advisors thoroughly and completely from the human consequences of the decisions they make. I do not believe that the president or Mr. [Secretary of State Dean] Rusk or Mr. [Secretary of Defense Robert] McNamara or even [National Security Advisor] McGeorge Bundy are particularly evil men. If asked to throw napalm on the back of a ten-year-old child they would shrink in horror—but their decisions have led to the mutilation and death of thousands and thousands of people.

What kind of system is it that allows good men to make those kinds of decisions? What kind of system is it that justifies the United States or any country seizing the destinies of the Vietnamese people and using them callously for its own purpose? What kind of system is it that disenfranchises people in the South, leaves millions upon millions of people throughout the country impoverished and excluded from the mainstream and promise of American society, that creates faceless and terrible bureaucracies and makes those the place where people spend their lives and do their work, that consistently puts material values before human values and still persists in

Photo on following page: A group of women and children are rounded up before being shot by U.S. soldiers in pursuit of Vietcong guerrillas in My Lai, South Vietnam. (**Ronald L. Haeberle/Contributor/ Time & Life Pictures/ Getty Images.**)

calling itself free and still persists in finding itself fit to police the world? What place is there for ordinary men in that system and how are they to control it, make it bend itself to their wills rather than bending them to its?

We must name that system. We must name it, describe it, analyze it, understand it and change it. For it is only when that system is changed and brought under control that there can be any hope for stopping the forces that create a war in Vietnam today or a murder in the South tomorrow or all the incalculable, innumerable more subtle atrocities that are worked on people all over all the time.

Building an Anti-War Movement

How do you stop a war then? If the war has its roots deep in the institutions of American society, how do you stop it? Do you march to Washington? Is that enough? Who will hear us? How can you make the decision makers hear us, insulated as they are, if they cannot hear the screams of a little girl burnt by napalm?

I believe that the administration is serious about expanding the war in Asia. The question is whether the people here are as serious about ending it. I wonder what it means for each of us to say we want to end the war in Vietnam—whether, if we accept the full meaning of that statement and the gravity of the situation, we can simply leave the march and go back to the routines of a society that acts as if it were not in the midst of a grave crisis. Maybe we, like the president, are insulated from the consequences of our own decision to end the war. Maybe we have yet really to listen to the screams of a burning child and decide that we cannot go back to whatever it is we did before today until that war has ended.

> If the people of this country are to end the war in Vietnam . . . then the people of this country must create a massive social movement.

There is no simple plan, no scheme or gimmick that can be proposed here. There is no simple way to attack something that is deeply rooted in the society. If the people of this country are to end the war in Vietnam, and to change the institutions which create it, then the people of this country must create a massive social movement— and if that can be built around the issue of Vietnam, then that is what we must do.

By a social movement I mean more than petitions or letters of protest, or tacit support of dissident congressmen; I mean people who are willing to change their lives, who are willing to challenge the system, to take the problem of change seriously. By a social movement I mean an effort that is powerful enough to make the country understand that our problems are not in Vietnam, or China or Brazil or outer space or at the bottom of the ocean, but are here in the United States. What we must do is begin to build a democratic and humane society in which Vietnams are unthinkable, in which human life and initiative are precious. The reason there are twenty thousand people here today and not a hundred or none at all is because five years ago in the South students began to build a social movement to change the system. The reason there are poor people, Negro and white, housewives, faculty members, and many others here in Washington is because that movement has grown and spread and changed and reached out as an expression of the broad concerns of people throughout the society. The reason the war and the system it represents will be stopped, if it is stopped before it destroys all of us, will be because the movement has become strong enough to exact change in the society. Twenty thousand people—the people here, if they were serious, if they were willing to break out of their isolation and to accept the consequences of a decision to end the war and commit themselves to building a movement wherever they are and in whatever way they effectively can—would be, I'm convinced, enough. . . .

For in a strange way the people of Vietnam and the people on this demonstration are united in much more than a common concern that the war be ended. In both countries there are people struggling to build a movement that has the power to change their condition. The system that frustrates these movements is the same. All our lives, our destinies, our very hopes to live, depend on our ability to overcome that system.

The United States Is an Imperialistic Force that Must Be Defeated

Ho Chi Minh

Ho Chi Minh established the Democratic Republic of Vietnam (North Vietnam) in 1945 and served as its leader until his death in 1969. During the period of French occupation after World War II, Minh headed the Viet Minh movement that fought French forces and ultimately led to the French withdrawal from the country in 1954. Regarded by many Vietnamese as a hero for his role in the fight against France, Ho was trusted and respected even by individuals in South Vietnam who fought against his army. In the following viewpoint, excerpted from a 1965 newspaper piece, Ho calls on the Vietnamese people to stand strong against the imperialistic U.S. invaders who seek to subjugate the country. He believes that his peoples' resolve will defeat the Americans and that eventually the U.S. forces will be expelled just as the French forces before them. While Ho has obvious disdain for the U.S. military and its tactics, he offers

SOURCE. Ho Chi Minh, *Vietnam and America*. New York: Grove, 1985. Reproduced by permission.

a word of friendship and solidarity for "progressive" Americans who oppose the unjust war that he claims they were duped into supporting.

Over the past ten years, the U.S. imperialists and their henchmen have carried out an extremely ruthless war and have caused much grief to our compatriots in South Vietnam. Over the past few months, they have frenziedly expanded the war to North Vietnam. In defiance of the 1954 Geneva Agreements and international law, they have sent hundreds of aircraft and dozens of warships to bomb and strafe North Vietnam repeatedly. Laying bare themselves their piratical face, the U.S. aggressors are blatantly encroaching upon our country. They hope that by resorting to the force of weapons they can compel our 30 million compatriots to become their slaves. But they are grossly mistaken. They will certainly meet with ignominious defeat.

The Resolve to Defeat the American Imperialists

Our Vietnamese people are a heroic people. Over the past ten years or more, our 14 million compatriots in the South have overcome all hardships, made every sacrifice and struggled very valiantly. Starting with their bare hands, they have seized guns from the enemy to fight against the enemy, have recorded victory after victory, and are launching a continual attack inflicting upon the U.S. aggressors and the traitors ever greater defeats and causing them to be bogged down more and more deeply. The greater their defeats, the more frantically they resort to the most cruel means, such as using napalm bombs and toxic gas to massacre our compatriots in the South. It is because they are bogged

> We love peace but we are not afraid of war.

down in South Vietnam that they have furiously attacked North Vietnam.

... The U.S. imperialists are precisely the saboteurs of the Geneva Agreements, yet they have brazenly declared that because they wished to "restore peace" and "defend the Geneva Agreements" they brought U.S. troops to our country to carry out massacres and destruction. ...

U.S. President [Lyndon] Johnson has . . . loudly threatened to resort to violence to subdue our people. This is a mere foolish illusion. Our people will definitely never be subjugated.

The Taylor plan has been frustrated. The McNamara plan has also gone bankrupt. The "escalation" plan which the U.S. imperialists are now endeavoring to carry out in North Vietnam will certainly fail, too. The U.S. imperialists may send in dozens of thousands more U.S. officers and men and make all-out efforts to drag more troops of their satellite countries into this criminal war, but our army and people are resolved to fight and defeat them. ...

Americans Have Been Duped

We love peace but we are not afraid of war. We are resolved to drive away the U.S. aggressors and to defend the freedom, independence, and territorial integrity of our Fatherland.

The people throughout our country are firmly confident that with their militant solidarity, valiant spirit, and creative wisdom, and with the sympathy and support of the world's peoples, they will certainly lead this great Resistance War to complete victory.

Our people are very grateful to and highly value the fraternal solidarity and devoted assistance of the socialist countries, especially the Soviet Union and China, of the people in all continents who are actively supporting us in our struggle against the U.S. imperialist aggressors, the most cruel enemy of mankind. ...

Nguyen Thi Binh: North Vietnam's Diplomat to the World

The most visible South Vietnamese Communist during the Vietnam War [was Nguyen Thi Binh]. Madame Binh, as she became known worldwide, served as diplomat for the National Liberation Front (NLF), the political wing of the Viet Cong insurrection, from 1962 to 1969 and as foreign minister to the Provisional Revolutionary Government (PRG), the NLF's successor, from 1969 to 1973.

As a diplomat for the NLF, Binh traveled around the world to publicize the cause of South Vietnamese communism and national reunification. She became a familiar figure in many Western countries and certainly the most well-known spokesperson for the NLF. In 1969 the PRG sent her, as foreign minister, to Paris, where peace negotiations among the North Vietnamese, South Vietnamese, and Americans were under way. As the official PRG representative, Binh sought to include the PRG in any potential new regime in South Vietnam. This proved to be a major sticking point in negotiations, since South Vietnamese president Nguyen Van Thieu did not want to share his power with Communists. She also tried to ensure that any release of American prisoners of war would coincide with the release of political prisoners held by the Saigon regime. When the Paris Peace Accords were finally settled in January 1973, Binh signed on behalf of the PRG, although Thieu refused to sign at the same time. After the reunification of Vietnam and the creation of the Socialist Republic of Vietnam in 1976, Binh went on to be one of the few southern officials to hold important posts in the Hanoi government. One of these was the vice presidency, in the early 1990s.

SOURCE. *Jeff T. Hay, "Nguyen Thi Binh,"* The Greenhaven Encyclopedia of the Vietnam War. *Ed. Charles Zappia. San Diego: Greenhaven, 2004.*

The American people have been duped by the propaganda of their government, which has extorted from them billions of dollars to throw into the crater of war. Thousands of American youths—their sons and brothers—have met a tragic death or have been pitifully wounded on the Vietnamese battlefields thousands of miles from the United States. At present, many mass organizations of individuals in the United States are demanding that their government at once stop this unjust war and withdraw U.S. troops from South Vietnam. Our people are resolved to drive away the U.S. imperialists, our sworn enemy. But we always express our friendship with the progressive American people. . . .

The Vietnamese Must Unify to Win the War

Our people are living in an extremely glorious period of history. Our country has the great honor of being an outpost of the socialist camp and of the world's peoples who are struggling against imperialism, colonialism, and neocolonialism.

Ho Chi Minh, leader of North Vietnam, accused the United States of breaking the 1954 Geneva Agreements by attacking his country unprovoked. (**Hulton Archive/ Stringer/Archive Photos/ Getty Images.**)

Our people have fought and made sacrifices not only for the sake of their own freedom and independence, but also for the common freedom and independence of the other peoples and for peace in the world.

On the battlefront against the U.S. aggressors, our people's task is very heavy but also very glorious. . . .

I call on our compatriots and fighters to constantly heighten their revolutionary heroism, vigilance, and fighting spirit—to promote the "everyone redoubles his efforts" emulation movement, resolutely overcome all difficulties, endeavor to build and defend socialist North Vietnam and wholeheartedly support the patriotic struggle of our compatriots in the South!

Let all of us single-mindedly unite as one man and be determined to defeat the U.S. aggressors!

For the future of our Fatherland, for the happiness of our people, let all compatriots and fighters throughout the country valiantly march forward!

The United States Must Stop Devastating Vietnam and Cease Its Involvement in Their Civil War

French and Japanese scientists

The following viewpoint is composed of two open letters endorsed, respectively, by 200 scientists from France and 1,300 scientists from Japan. The French letter is addressed to the American scientific community, calling on those scientists who oppose the war in Vietnam to continue resisting. The French scientists claim that their own country's experience fighting popular-front guerrilla movements in both Algeria and Vietnam has taught them that negotiation, not destruction, is the path to peace. The Japanese letter calls on the Japanese

---

SOURCE. "Vietnam Statements by Scientists Abroad," *Bulletin of the Atomic Scientists*, vol. 23, January 1967, pp. 47–48. Copyright © 1967 by the Educational Foundation for Nuclear Science, Chicago, IL 60637. Reproduced by permission of *Bulletin of the Atomic Scientists: The Magazine of Global Security News & Analysis*.

government to renege on its agreements with the United States to provide military bases for U.S. aircraft heading for Vietnam. According to the Japanese scientists, America's unjust and aggressive involvement in a Vietnamese civil war makes the treaty provisions null and void. Both letters were forwarded to the *Bulletin of the Atomic Scientists*, where they were published in January 1967.

An Open Letter from French Scientists

Many of us, French physicists and mathematicians, know you personally and your country very well through years of residence on American campuses and in American research institutions. All of us have been impressed by the sense of responsibility and the courage to face the hard facts about Vietnam displayed by a large part of the American scientific community. Moreover, we ourselves have had a long and painful involvement in wars against newly-emerging countries, in particular with Vietnam and Algeria. For all these reasons, we wish to let you know our feelings on the present situation.

Although they are no longer making headlines, the hideous methods used to strike an enemy who is hiding among and deriving support from the population are afflicting every human conscience: napalm, chemical and gas warfare, burning of villages, torture. We have seen our own country doing the same sort of things and wish we had done more to oppose it. Now it is carried out with the aid of modern technology and on a larger scale. How far have we come from the 1924 Geneva Convention?

A dirty war in the South and, for more than a year now, systematic bombing of North Vietnam. The situation reminds us of the vain attempts of our own governments to fight the Algerian guerrilla war outside Algeria, at its "sources," Egypt and Tunisia. Remember that achieving this purpose was the main French motivation behind the Suez expedition. Remember too, the bombing

of the Tunisian village of Sakhiet: one school destroyed and a general uproar throughout the world, in particular, and justifiably enough, in the U.S. Given the number of air raids carried out over North Vietnam from above the clouds and with high speed bombers, how many Sakhiets can one estimate to be committed *every day now*?

One of the main stumbling blocks on the road to a solution seems to be the insistence of the U.S. government on dismissing the National Liberation Front [NLF] as a responsible agent, a reminder of the position held for

Algerian nationalist soldiers train along the Tunisian border in 1962. French physicists found many parallels between the United States' position in Vietnam and France's history with Algeria. **(Hank Walker/ Contributor/Time & Life Pictures/Getty Images.)**

many years by French governments toward the Vietminh and the Algerian NLF. It would take too long to retrace the recent history of Vietnam, but we wish to assert that, from all the sources available to us, there emerges a picture of the NLF [i.e., the Viet Cong] as a revolutionary movement enjoying the support of at least a large fraction of the South Vietnamese people. Another large fraction of the population, including representative religious communities, though not belonging to the NLF, oppose the successive governments which are supposed to control or represent them. Whatever our judgments may be on the past or future of Vietnam or on the political implications of a settlement there, we all find it hard to understand by what right a country can be brought to ashes in order to maintain in power a succession of puppet governments.

> We all find it hard to understand by what right a country can be brought to ashes in order to maintain in power a succession of puppet governments.

The French wars in Indochina and Algeria lasted for seven years each. In Indochina we were beaten on the field, in Algeria we reached a sort of military stalemate. In both cases we had to sit down with the leaders of the guerrilla movements, and our governments, after years of mistakes and uncertainty, found the wisdom to stop the fighting and eventually negotiated with the leaders of the Vietminh and the Algerian NLF. In the present situation also, we fear that a long time will be needed before the U.S. government will come to terms with reality, if indeed the conflict does not escalate into a third world war. Hence, we appreciate all the more the inspired efforts of many of you American scholars to put an end to the war in Vietnam. And with this letter, we wish to convey our deep sympathy and express our active support for your endeavor.

A Statement by Japanese Physicists

The war in Vietnam is being escalated. Despite powerful opposition from world public opinion, the United States is continuing its bombing of North Vietnam, and is turning South Vietnam into a devastated land through the use of napalm bombs and poisonous gas. The war is thus expanding in scope and degree, making us feel keenly the danger that American-Chinese hostilities will break out.

The government of the USA claims that aggression from the North is the cause of the war and that it has deployed its troops to Vietnam at the request of the South Vietnamese government. However, despite all these assertions, we cannot but conclude that the action of the United States in Vietnam constitutes an unjustified interference in the civil war of another country and an outright violation of the 1954 Geneva Agreement.

The Geneva Agreement of 1954, which drew a line of demarcation along the 17th parallel, at the same time clearly stated that it was but a temporary demarcation line and never was to be a political or territorial frontier. The Agreement guarantees the unity and sovereignty of Vietnam and prohibits military interference by foreign countries. The South Vietnamese government, backed militarily by the U.S. government, sabotaged united, free elections in Vietnam and cruelly repressed the people who advocated unification of their country. It was to resist this repression and to achieve one Vietnam that the South Vietnam National Liberation Front (NLF; the so-called Vietcong) was organized. It is reported that the National Liberation Front now controls three quarters of South Vietnam's territory.

> On no grounds is it tolerable that a foreign country arbitrarily intervenes in Vietnamese affairs.

It is to be deplored that, due to differences of opinion among the Vietnamese, a civil war has thus occurred in South Vietnam. However, the civil war is by all means the internal affair of the Vietnamese people. On no grounds is it tolerable that a foreign country arbitrarily intervenes in Vietnamese affairs, obstructs the unification of the nation, and destroys the life and culture of the Vietnamese people.

We are convinced that the Vietnam question should be settled by, and only by, the Vietnamese people themselves, including the NLF. We insist that to enable the Vietnamese people to settle their affairs, it is vitally essential that the United States should stop its belligerent action, including aerial attacks on North Vietnam, and withdraw all of its troops from Vietnam.

The Japanese government, on its part, is playing the role of an accomplice in the present war, by offering, under the U.S.-Japan Security Treaty, Japanese territory as operational bases for U.S. troops. Such a policy runs counter to the will of the overwhelming majority of the peaceloving Japanese people. We demand, on the above mentioned grounds, that the Japanese government immediately discard its present policy with respect to the Vietnam war.

We, Japanese physicists, urge our friends in the United States to support this statement and to take appropriate action to change the Vietnam policy of the U.S. government.

Television and Print Journalism Eventually Turn Public Opinion Against the War

Andrew J. Huebner

In the following viewpoint, Andrew J. Huebner, a history professor at the University of Alabama, dispels commonplace notions that the American media in the 1960s was consistently skeptical of the justness and progress of the war in Vietnam. As Huebner explains, many news organs—both in print and on television—were fed information from Washington that they simply passed on to the public; others were as optimistic as the common citizen that the war against communism could be won in the early years. What eventually turned the tide, Huebner notes, is the fact that unrestricted access to battlefields and soldiers allowed news journalists to show fighting men pushed to their

SOURCE. Andrew J. Huebner, "Rethinking American Press Coverage of the Vietnam War, 1965–68," *Journalism History*, vol. 31, Fall 2005. Reproduced by permission of the publisher and author.

limits, frightened for their lives, and often doubtful of their superiors and the overall strategy of the war. Coupled with the broadcast of disturbing images—such as the burning of enemy villages and the pain and injury of soldiers and civilians—these firsthand reports showed the people of the United States the savage cost of war in ways the public had not experienced in previous conflicts.

In the early 1960s a handful of journalists, including David Halberstam, Neil Sheehan, Malcolm Browne, and Peter Arnett, were covering what still seemed a distant and murky conflict. Under President John Kennedy, the United States increased the number of advisers it sent to assist the South Vietnamese regime in its struggle against the communist forces of the National Liberation Front (NLF), or Vietcong, and their allies in communist North Vietnam. The early print reporters strongly supported the presence of American advisers in Vietnam but increasingly questioned the likelihood of defeating the communists. Stories in the *New York Times*—and Halberstam's 1965 book *The Making of a Quagmire*—depicted a determined enemy, unmotivated and poorly trained South Vietnamese soldiers, and American officials who grasped neither the political nature of the war nor the unsuitability of massive military power to such a conflict. Just as the correspondents in Vietnam recognized the disastrous geopolitical consequences of an American withdrawal, they also foresaw trouble if the United States upped its commitment. With great prescience, Halberstam in his book contemplated the costs of sending American soldiers to Vietnam: "Whatever military gains were brought by U.S. troops might soon be countered by the political loss. . . . It would be a war without fronts, fought against an elusive enemy, and extremely difficult for the American people to understand." Despite such warnings, in the years after

Kennedy's assassination in 1963, the [President Lyndon] Johnson administration escalated the war, culminating in the commitment of ground troops to protect the American airbase at Danang in March 1965.

The Media as an Ally of the White House

With large numbers of American boys now in harm's way, Vietnam had turned from a back-page news story into what the *New Yorker*'s Michael Arlen later called "a central fact in American life." By 1965, there were print journalists in Vietnam representing four magazines (*Life*, *Look*, *Time*, and *Newsweek*), two wire services (the Associated Press and United Press International), and several newspapers (notably the *New York Times* and *Washington Post*). Halberstam, Sheehan, Browne, Arnett, Bernard Fall, Stanley Karnow, and others distinguished themselves covering the war in print. Prominent photographers in Vietnam included David Douglas Duncan, Carl Mydans, Larry Burrows, Eddie Adams, Horst Faas, Dickey

> Vietnam is better remembered as the first televised war.

Chapelle, and military cameraman Ronald Haeberle. Large, color photographs in *Life* and other periodicals, sitting on coffee tables in waiting rooms throughout the United States during the Vietnam era, comprised a large part of the war's visual legacy.

Yet Vietnam is better remembered as the first televised war. "Most of us knew about it, felt about it, from television," wrote Arlen. Each of the three main networks had correspondents in Vietnam by 1965. CBS and NBC lengthened their nightly news programs from fifteen to thirty minutes in 1963, and ABC did so in 1967, allowing more time for coverage of the war in Vietnam. Televised dispatches arrived in American living rooms from correspondents who would go on to prominent careers in journalism: Ed Bradley, Garrick Utley, Ted Koppel, Morley Safer, Dan Rather, and Mike Wallace. The network studio anchors—Walter Cronkite, Chet Huntley, David Brinkley, Peter Jennings, and others—shepherded the field reports from Vietnam to the American public. After the Tet offensive of 1968, some anchors became increasingly critical of the war (Cronkite famously pronounced Vietnam a "stalemate" on February 27, 1968), but through 1967 these men tended to present the news with little interpretation.

Indeed, as Susan Moeller has pointed out in her book on combat photography, these publications and television networks were institutions of the "establishment media." They considered themselves allies of the White House even when their correspondents in the field sent back pessimistic reports about the war. In the early period after American ground troops arrived in country—from March 1965 through 1967—even those journalists who questioned American methods in Vietnam rarely challenged the American presence there (as some reporters had during the Kennedy years). The media, like the public, generally supported Cold War anticommunism and approved of the American intervention in Vietnam. Lest television viewers had forgotten the threat, hanging on the wall behind Cronkite's desk on the CBS nightly newscast was a map of Vietnam with "RED CHINA" looming to the north.

Nevertheless, during the Vietnam War there was considerable—and unprecedented—room for dissent among the press corps. While censorship of press coverage had prevailed during World War II and in the Korean War by 1951, no official control of the media occurred at any point during the Vietnam War. With all of the technological advances of the 1960s, particularly television and satellites, military officials simply could not imagine censoring the news. [Overall U.S. commander] Gen. William Westmoreland, for example,

The My Lai Massacre

At 7:40 on the morning of 16 March 1968, Charlie Company [of the U.S. 23rd Infantry Division] landed on the outskirts of My Lai [South Vietnam], where its assignment was to sweep through the village and eliminate all Vietcong resistance. . . . The company was frustrated and angry. It had suffered losses through booby traps, mines, and snipers, and its demoralization began to show up in increasingly brutal behavior while on routine missions.

The First Platoon, led by Lieutenant William L. Calley, began moving through the village to flush out the enemy. They were operating under the faulty intelligence that all villagers would be at market at this time and that anyone they found would by default be Vietcong. As the platoon pushed on, Calley's men began a rampage of indiscriminate killing. The troops shot mothers and their babies, they shot the elderly, and they raped girls and young women before killing them. Terrified and panicked, many villagers tried to flee but were summarily rounded up into holding groups and shot at point-blank range. . . .

The massacre of civilians at My Lai generally drew little attention at task force headquarters. Murmurs of disapproval were quickly squashed in a cover-up that reached high up the chain of command. . . .

On 13 November 1969, however, the incident moved out of military jurisdiction and into the public realm: the journalist Seymour Hersh broke the story in newspapers around the country. On 5 December, *Life* magazine printed a grisly series of photographs taken during the massacre by Ron Haeberle, who was on active service with Charlie Company as an army photographer.

The My Lai exposé triggered outrage across the country. Those in favor of the war saw the story as another attempt to tear the United States down, while those opposed to the war claimed it was added proof that the military was morally bankrupt and the war was moving into a genocidal phase.

SOURCE. *Paul Hanson, "My Lai Massacre,"* Violence in America. *Ed. Ronald Gottesman. New York: Charles Scribner's Sons, 1999.*

believed the logistics of censorship were "forbidding to contemplate."

Managed News Reports

Some methods of control, however, did restrict reporters in Vietnam. Members of the media often faced official requests to withhold news of troop movements and graphic depictions of the dead and wounded. Reporters whom the military leadership in Vietnam did not favor might be denied transportation to the countryside, official accreditation, interviews with commanders, or lodging at military bases. And the brass could, as always, hold back or distort the information it released to the press. For years the military's public information officers in Saigon held the much-derided "Five-O'clock Follies," a daily briefing that provided the official version of the war. Indeed, many stories from news agencies during the Vietnam War relied on information provided by military and administration representatives. And television networks had their own policies governing the release of footage that might disturb families of the dead and wounded.

In short, there were numerous informal ways the military and government could manage the news, but early in the war the press usually fell into line of its own volition. Eventually journalists in Vietnam took advantage of the lack of official censorship and delivered more critical war reporting. After the Tet offensive of early 1968 the tenor of press coverage in Vietnam became more skeptical, and the impact of that change on administration policy and public opinion became the subject of an extensive, highly partisan debate for decades afterwards.

The Image of the Pitiable Hero

Yet if journalists generally supported American involvement in Indochina early in the war, that did not inhibit them from propagating troubling depictions of the GI.

Between 1965 and 1968 the media, particularly popular magazines and television networks, trotted out manifold versions of the foot soldier, some of which coexisted awkwardly with editorial support for the war. The upshot was a bewildering set of portraits of soldiers and of the war effort generally which was a "constant flow of words and images" bringing "obfuscation," not "clarification," according to *The New York*'s noted correspondent Robert Shaplen.

Reporters began by emphasizing the skill, toughness, commitment, and compassion of the American fighting man, which were images dusted off from World War II. But quickly the flavor of Korean War coverage tempered those characterizations, with GIs seeming to be increasingly victimized by combat, the elements, their superiors, and gradually the very presence of the American military in Vietnam. The heroic, selfless soldier of World War II mythology was gradually transforming into a different sort of cultural hero, one inviting sympathy, even pity, along with adoration. The terms of what made a soldier honorable—indeed, the terms of what made him a man—were widening and changing. So when coverage of the Tet offensive in early 1968 delivered what seemed to be startling imagery of the war and the American GI, it was more intense but not new.

> Reporters began by emphasizing the skill, toughness, commitment, and compassion of the American fighting man, which were images dusted off from World War II.

Though the Vietnam War is better remembered for a breakdown in military discipline after 1970, in the early period of the war reporters lauded the efficiency, teamwork, and might of the American armed forces. This image of professionalism was a natural one given the high proportion of professional or volunteer soldiers (compared to draftees) in the country. Invoking a theme that had dominated coverage of World War II, the press once again placed individual soldiers within the framework of a well-oiled machine. . . .

Doubts Arise About Soldiers' Preparedness for Guerrilla Warfare

Alongside consistent praise of the GIs, however, a few whispers of doubt circulated in 1965 about the ability of the American military to handle guerrilla warfare. Some media reports—and they were rare at this point—hinted that American troops were having trouble with the guerrillas. *Newsweek* reported as early as July 1965 that officials in Washington were "embarrassed" by the performance of Marines guarding the Danang air base. Responding to questions about a damaging Vietcong raid on the position, a testy Pentagon official responded, "I wish we'd quit blaming the South Vietnamese for these incidents."

Life sent a similar message in more measured tones when it reported ten days later that "U.S. combat units are finding that they still have a lot to learn about guerrilla warfare." The article went on to charge that American troops were making the same "mistakes" advisers had rebuked the South Vietnamese for in previous years; namely, they were relying too heavily on logistically complicated and time-consuming air strikes. *Newsweek* worried in August 1965 that if the Americans kept up their deadly air war against the Vietcong and North Vietnamese, they would soon find themselves in the position of the French colonizers of an earlier era: "alien intruders feared and hated by the general population." ABC correspondent Malcolm Browne, when asked in November whether American GIs were prepared to fight and win in Vietnam, replied, "Frankly, I don't think they are. I think these boys are magnificently trained to fight World War II and fight Korea, but I think this is a different kind of conflict. In this kind of war, politics and economics and a lot of other factors are important." Such depictions did not question the professionalism or courage of GIs but their ability to get the job done in the particular locale of Vietnam.

The Cam Ne Incident

One of the war's most enduring and controversial images of GIs arrived in American living rooms in August 1965, just weeks after Johnson boosted his administration's military commitment to South Vietnam. In an early execution of the "search and destroy" strategy, Marines entered the hamlet of Cam Ne on August 3. CBS correspondent Safer reported that Vietcong troops were "long gone" from the alleged enemy stronghold by the time the GIs arrived. Nevertheless, the soldiers had orders to destroy the village, and the CBS camera crew recorded

> The Pentagon . . . began recording nightly television coverage of Vietnam to keep an eye on the networks.

infamous footage of Americans using Zippo lighters to set thatched huts on fire. "There is little doubt that American fire power can win a military victory here," Safer commented. "But to a Vietnamese peasant whose home means a lifetime of backbreaking labor, it will take more than presidential promises to convince him that we are on his side." His report exposed, quite early, two chronic difficulties of the war in Vietnam: differentiating villagers from soldiers and winning over the South Vietnamese population in the face of substantial civilian casualties.

Not surprisingly, the president and the military leaders were furious about the story on Cam Ne. In an oft-quoted telephone call, Johnson asked CBS president Frank Stanton, "Are you trying to f--- me?" Angry enough that Safer was a Canadian, administration officials also wondered if he might be a communist, and officials in the White House and the Department of Defense

CBS News correspondent Morley Safer reports on the burning of South Vietnamese homes by U.S. soldiers in Cam Ne on August 3, 1965. The Vietnam War is widely considered to be the first televised war. (CBS Photo Archive/ Contributor/CBS/Getty Images.)

tried unsuccessfully to pressure CBS into withdrawing him from his assignment. The Pentagon also began recording nightly television coverage of Vietnam to keep an eye on the networks. Scholars rightly have pointed out that Safer's dispatch was unusual in 1965—otherwise why the irate reaction?—but the furor it caused surely inflated its impact. As [historian] Tom Engelhardt put it, Safer's images "were perhaps the most disturbing of the war for those who saw them that August night," precisely because they broke the mold of prior television coverage. . . .

Conflicting Images of American Intervention

As scholar Chester Pach has noted, after the furor over Cam Ne, Safer's dispatches tended to blame warfare, not the GIs, for the death of civilians (Safer spoke in late August of "the inevitable civilian suffering" in war). In this case he went even further, indicating that American soldiers were protecting South Vietnamese villagers from the Vietcong and from American firepower. Such was "censorship" in the Vietnam context; consciously or otherwise, he issued more encouraging reports after LBJ's [Lyndon Johnson's] intimidating outburst. Other correspondents did so as well; in the same period NBC's Utley issued a dispatch with footage of American GIs aiding women who had been tortured by the Vietcong.

These two messages—that American GIs might hurt civilians but also might help them—appeared nearly side-by-side in an NBC report by Dean Brelis that aired on August 30. He began his dispatch with grim words accompanying footage of bedraggled Vietnamese refugees. These people had been displaced partly because of "Vietcong terrorism" but also because "Americans have turned their villages and farms into a battleground." Yet that did not mean, as he said and images showed, that the civilians were worse off for their contact with the Americans. On the contrary, "[M]ore than Marine guns, Marine heart has helped [the refugees]. . . . In the same volunteer spirit, the Marines donate medical supplies to the village dispensary." Meanwhile, Navy doctors entered the area to provide medical services to the villagers, "not as part of orders, but because they want to help the living."

Some of the doubts circulating in the media earlier in 1965 subsided when the American presence—185,000 strong by the end of the year—seemed to stabilize South Vietnam. In October, *Time* wrote with no shortage of drama of the "remarkable turnabout" in the country, a place that now "throbs with a pride and power, above all an *esprit*, scarcely credible against the summer's somber vista." Of course, not all was rosy. *Time* reported in January 1966 that 1,241 Americans had died in Vietnam in 1965 and 5,687 were wounded. But as Cronkite announced, quoting Secretary of Defense Robert McNamara on the evening of November 29, "We have stopped losing the war." It was a fitting expression of progress in a perplexing conflict. . . .

Differing Portrayals of GIs

Popular magazines continued in 1966 to illustrate the professionalism, efficiency, and compassion of American GIs. *Newsweek* pointed out in August 1966 that fewer than 25 percent of soldiers in Vietnam were draftees, though it presciently predicted an increase in that figure. As in the previous year, journalists in 1966 often countered the idea that American GIs posed a threat to the civilians of South Vietnam, highlighting instead the positive impact of the Americans on ordinary Vietnamese. . . .

Not all coverage of the GI in 1966, however, touted his professionalism, compassion, and competence. Nor did popular news agencies ignore death and injury in wartime. Alongside the growth of domestic antiwar sentiment, the complexities of war and the soldier's reaction to it crept steadily into news coverage of Vietnam.

The American military occasionally made mistakes, and the press reported these in a frank manner. In January a televised dispatch from CBS correspondent Rather showed panicky GIs running for cover under fire, while the company commander frantically tried to call off what he assumed to be his own artillery. The barrage, in fact, came from the enemy, but the quick assumption that it was American indicated the frequency of error. Indeed, later estimates suggested that as many as 20 percent of all American casualties came from friendly fire.

In November, a CBS camera crew caught just such a moment of error on film. As poorly aimed air strikes rained down on the GIs, one screamed into his radio: "Get the damn thing away from me! That's landing right in us!" Though correspondent Bruce Morton noted that most air support was devastatingly effective, the image of the shouting GI may have overwhelmed that fact. A similar phenomenon marked an article in *Time* that fall. The text reported that American pilots had accidentally napalmed their own GIs, though the division commander of the unit "held no grudges" and said he would call in the air strikes again if necessary. . . .

Depicting the Costs of War

Unlike in years past, however, some publications now put images of the wounded onto their covers. Starting with an issue in July 1965, *Life* put injured GIs in this prominent position several times. In February and October of 1966, *Life* covers showed soldiers in particularly helpless states, with bandaged faces and ragged, torn clothing. Inside the February 11 issue, several photographs from the same series showed a medic, who was "so completely bandaged that he could barely peer out of one eye," feeding C-rations to another soldier with a head wound. The pictures expressed American compassion as few other images could, and the wounded GIs surely invited deep sympathy. Another victim of the war, a Marine south of the Demilitarized Zone (DMZ), appeared unconscious, his head swathed in bandages, on *Life's* cover of October 28. An article on the military situation in *Newsweek* in April included a large picture of Lt. Richard Lindsey, hit by shrapnel and crying in pain. Though they were by no means daily fare on television, nightly news stories in 1966 occasionally showed interviews with wounded American

> "Deliberate or inadvertent abuse of civilians, Vietcong prisoners, and enemy suspects continued to command significant attention."

soldiers, footage of grimacing GIs, and on-screen medical procedures.

Such images were not necessarily "antiwar"; journalists surely understood that wounds and death were a part of any conflict. But these images conveyed a picture of war that reminded viewers of its costs. In this way reporters valorized the suffering of the individual GI, and made him seem pitiable, but without questioning his manliness or toughness. As Moeller has written, combat photographers in Vietnam "took portraits of the troops to champion the fortitude of the individual soldiers in their sad triumph over the hardship of warfare."

Torture and Brutality

Deliberate or inadvertent abuse of civilians, Vietcong prisoners, and enemy suspects continued to command significant attention. Sometimes such treatment seemed justified. Rather reported from Vietnam in January 1966:

> In this village along the Saigon riverbanks, residents admit a Vietcong battalion, with Chinese advisers, spent the night, moving out just a few hours before U.S. troops came in. Our troops continue burning every hut they find, and all crops, convinced that practically every man, woman, and child in this section belongs to the Vietcong.

Laura Bergquist of *Look* suggested just how tragic this thinking could be for the people of South Vietnam:

> A visit to the jungle that is the Da Nang Surgical Hospital brings on nausea. There, two to a bed, lie hideously wounded Vietnamese civilians, children and adults. Eighty percent are war victims (mostly mortar and mine wounds, ours and Vietcong Charlie's). I couldn't look at one child, perhaps seven, who was one huge, blistered napalm wound.

In the spring, newspapers around the country ran a photograph by Sean Flynn of a Vietcong sniper strung up in a tree by his heels. *Time* lamented the widespread attention the photograph garnered, particularly since most publications ran it without his accompanying dispatch

AGE OF U.S. MILITARY PERSONNEL KILLED IN THE VIETNAM WAR	
Age at Time of Death/Declaration of Death	**Number of Records**
17	12
18	3,103
19	8,283
20	14,095
21	9,705
22	4,798
23	3,495
24	2,650
25	2,018
26	1,414
27	917
28	768
29	710
30–39	4,927
40–49	1,156
50–59	121
60–62	4
Unknown, not reported	17
Total	**58,193**

Source: National Archives, Statistical Information About Casualties of the Vietnam War. www.archives.gov.

about how the prisoner had killed a baby and was cut down unharmed after only fifteen minutes. "Such pictures," groaned the magazine, "are hardly ever balanced out by coverage of the Viet Cong's far more common tactics of terror and brutality." Evidence of American or South Vietnamese harshness "so often" received undue coverage with "indignant captions." Trying to right the wrong, perhaps, *Time* had recently reported on the killing and mutilation of two American pilots by the Vietcong. Dispatches on the brutality of the enemy often appeared in this context, as if to help justify images of American cruelty. . . .

> Also intensifying during Vietnam was the sense that the GI might be a victim of overly sanguine or even deceitful leadership.

Bitterness and Mistrust

In 1967 the press intensified its use of imagery that had circulated since 1965 and would be popularly associated with the looming Tet offensive. More and more, American GIs were shown to be bitter about their situation in Vietnam, resentful of the brass, and even emotionally scarred by combat, which was the hallmark of Vietnam imagery in subsequent popular mythology. . . .

Also intensifying during Vietnam was the sense that the GI might be a victim of overly sanguine or even deceitful leadership. Widely associated with the Tet offensive, critiques of military officials had far deeper roots. As [historian Daniel] Hallin rightly pointed out, 1967 saw stirrings of doubt in the press corps, but they appeared in small hints even before that during the Vietnam War.

In his report from Con Thien, [CBS reporter Robert] Schakne interviewed Major Gordon Cook, commander of the Marines stationed there. Cook admitted that the GIs "don't have too much flexibility as far as moving out of here," but he brusquely dismissed comparisons to the doomed French garrison at Dien Bien Phu in 1954: "I don't feel in any way, shape, or form that this is anything like Dien Bien Phu. This is a complete connotation that is erroneous, and I don't want anybody to think we're in this position. We're in a good position here. I feel pretty confident, frankly." Another officer cheerfully declared that he would be able to get his men all the supplies they needed by helicopter, despite widespread reports on the difficulties of flying aircraft into the DMZ area. If the gap between these assurances and the interviews with GIs was not obvious enough, Schakne concluded his report with words and footage that clashed with official optimism:

> On this day, forty-three wounded Marines were brought out of Con Thien. Some of them had to lie on stretchers for over two hours before the helicopters could come in and get them and take them out. They had to wait through one ten-minute barrage of over one hundred shells. This is the way it is, this is the way it's been, and this is the way it's going to be for quite a while at Con Thien.

When the network cut back to Cronkite, the esteemed anchor said journalists returning from the DMZ were describing Marine losses much heavier than the military was reporting. "And today," he intoned, "the U.S. command ordered sharp restrictions on information that is given out about the communist shellings." Though he purportedly lost faith in the American war only after the Tet offensive of early 1968, on the evening of September 25, 1967, he described a widening gap between image and reality in Vietnam. . . .

Despite official protests, reporters at the DMZ painted a bleak picture. American GIs were demoralized, dirty, tired, scared, hungry, thirsty, and often wounded or killed. Occasionally they seemed skeptical of their superiors, and official accounts of the fighting often contradicted impressions given by interviews with individual GIs. In short, the American soldier seemed a stoic victim of forces far beyond his control. The power of the military seemed particularly ominous during a CBS broadcast in April 1967. A military official interviewed by Wallace, when asked whether the American people would accept projected losses of 25,000 dead, replied, "Do they have any choice?"

By the end of 1967, with 486,000 American troops in Vietnam, the war was at an impasse. Despite suffering crushing losses, there were no signs that the enemy's will was breaking. Neither the North Vietnamese nor the Americans were willing to de-escalate unless the other side did so first. Johnson vowed at Christmas to no longer expect the enemy to honor overtures of peace. "A burned child dreads the fire," the president said, in what was surely one of his most ill-chosen metaphors of the war.

In September, CBS broadcast more words from the president. Grieving for the casualties of war—in that year, 9,378 Americans died in Vietnam, almost doubling the number of deaths in 1966—Johnson said, "No one hates war and killing more than I do. No sane American can greet the news from Vietnam with enthusiasm." Given the grimness of imagery in 1967, few Americans, even the tenuous majority still supportive of the war, could muster enthusiasm for the news. "We want to tell people what this war is like," CBS' Schakne told *Newsweek* in a year-end article on television coverage of Vietnam. "It's nothing like a John Wayne movie."

On January 30, 1968, more than 70,000 communist troops launched coordinated attacks on at least 100 cities and towns in South Vietnam, including Saigon, Khe Sanh, and the ancient city of Hué. The seemingly desperate NLF and North Vietnamese forces achieved almost total surprise, violating a temporary truce in observance of Tet, the Lunar New Year. After the initial shock wore off, the Americans and South Vietnamese inflicted enormous and often irrevocable losses on the enemy, which was reported by the news magazines, albeit alongside bloody and discouraging pictures. Although the communists paid dearly for the Tet offensive, they did succeed in further shrinking Johnson's credibility at home. As Karnow put it, surprised American television viewers suddenly saw "a drastically different kind of war"—or in Engelhardt's phrase, Tet sparked a "home front televisual disaster."

Depicting the Complexities of the Soldiers in Vietnam

It was true that urban combat and coordinated enemy attacks were novel elements in a war that had seemed, to American audiences, an endless string of jungle patrols. Yet much of what Americans saw and read of the war during Tet and thereafter reiterated, if more intensely, elements of media coverage between 1965 and 1968.

The infamous footage of the South Vietnamese general Nguyen Ngoc Loan shooting a bound Vietcong prisoner in 1968 surely sickened millions as had no earlier image. Americans were no less disturbed in the following year when *Life* published photographs of South Vietnamese villagers massacred by GIs in the hamlet of My Lai. Yet close observers of the news between 1965 and 1968 would have long suspected that the United States and its ally were guilty of such offenses, if not on the scale of My Lai or with the boldness of Loan. A reporter was wounded on camera during the Tet offensive, contributing to the abiding sense of chaos surrounding the attack, but the same thing had happened during a television broadcast in April 1967. When, during Tet, an American soldier told a reporter on camera, "The whole thing stinks, really," he was only repeating more starkly what GIs at Con Thien had been saying for months. Frightened villagers shown in dispatches after

1968 evoked earlier images from Safer's Cam Ne report. At the same time, during and after the Tet offensive TV news continued to see evidence of American compassion toward the Vietnamese people, bravery in combat, and professional skill.

In brief, much early coverage of the Vietnam War, like the admittedly grimmer and more critical reporting after the Tet offensive, did not characterize combat as mere romantic adventure. Journalists covering the conflict described a wide range of behaviors and attitudes among American GIs. Almost from the moment those soldiers started humping through the jungles of South Vietnam, journalists publicized their acts of bravery and cruelty, feelings of loneliness and comradeship and bitterness, and expressions of patriotism and manliness. These reporters have drawn widespread criticism from two opposite poles—one arguing the media showed too much, the other claiming they did not show nearly enough. Yet a close examination of what they wrote, photographed, and televised shows that journalists, in fact, produced a body of work that faithfully reflected the complexities and perplexities of the American fighting man and the war in Vietnam.

The United States Has Waged a Criminal and Imperialistic War in Vietnam

Shingo Shibata

Throughout the Vietnam War, millions of Vietnamese from both the North and the South were killed or wounded. Taking these numbers into account and considering the complete destruction of thousands of acres of land and cities, Shingo Shibata argues that the U.S. forces in Vietnam were imperialistic war criminals. Shibata presents statistics detailing the enormous tonnage of bombs dropped by the United States, the length of the war, the use of chemical weapons, and the needless loss of life to support his indictment of U.S. leaders and their government. Shingo Shibata was a Japanese professor, author, and philosopher who adamantly opposed the war in Vietnam.

SOURCE. Shingo Shibata, *Philosophical Currents 6: Lessons of the Vietnam War: Philosophical Considerations on the Vietnam Revolution.* B.R. Gruner, 1973. Reproduced by permission of the author.

O n January 27, 1973, an "Agreement on Ending the War and Restoring Peace in Vietnam" was signed by the Government of the Democratic Republic of Vietnam, the Government of the U.S.A., the Provisional Revolutionary Government of the Republic of South Vietnam, and the Saigon Administration. This represents a historic victory won by the Vietnamese people and the anti-imperialist democratic forces of the world who have stood on their side. . . .

No doubt, the signing of this agreement by no means amounts to the final solution to the problem of Vietnam. It still leaves a number of difficult problems to be settled by the Vietnamese people, especially by the people of South Vietnam and their Provisional Revolutionary Government. A new form of difficult struggle has just begun. What should be done to support this struggle, and further advance our own struggle in solidarity with the peoples of Vietnam, Laos and Cambodia? To find a proper answer to this question, it is necessary to recognize again what the war in Vietnam has meant. By so doing, we will be able to draw lessons from this war for our struggle ahead. . . .

An Unprecedented War of Aggression

The war in Vietnam was a war of aggression carried on by U.S. imperialism, the largest and the strongest ever seen in history, assaulting Vietnam with all its strength. U.S. imperialism put in action the largest and the most sophisticated air power, unprecedented in world history, and dropped an astronomical quantity of bombs and toxic chemicals. During World War II, the U.S. Forces dropped a total of about 2.06 million tons of bombs on Europe and in the Pacific, but the total amount of bombs used

> World history contains no such war record except the Vietnam war, that involved the use of such an amount of bombs, toxic chemicals, poison gases, and sophisticated antipersonnel weapons.

on Indochina from 1965 till the end of 1972 reached 7.70 million tons.

With shells added to these, the total amount of ammunition used by far exceeds 15 million tons, which is equivalent to more than 770 of the Hiroshima-type bombs being dropped in Indochina. By the use of toxic chemicals, the U.S. Forces by the end of 1970 had devastated 44% of forest zones plus 43% of farming areas. World history contains no such war record except the Vietnam war, that involved the use of such an amount of bombs, toxic chemicals, poison gases, and sophisticated antipersonnel weapons. Even according to a very conservative estimate worked out by a Cornell University team, more than one million of the civilian population were either killed or wounded, and an additional six million civilians, one third of the entire population, were made refugees in South Vietnam from 1965 through April 1971. The world has never experienced any war in which the crime of "genocide" was committed so openly and calculatedly. Bombing and shelling by the U.S. Forces were carried on in a manner calculated to kill all living things on the earth and even to destroy the ecological cycle and nature itself. Air and water reserves have been polluted, with even the temperature changed in some areas. Such terms as "biocide" and "ecocide" were coined, and indeed even these terms still fall far short of properly describing the atrocious nature of this war. . . .

If the war in Vietnam is regarded as having been fought ever since 1945, when French imperialism launched re-aggression against Vietnam with the support of U.S. imperialism, then it has gone on for over 28 years now (including a very short-lived "peace" following the 1954 Geneva agreements). Even taking the war as having been fought from 1961 when the U.S. launched its full-scale "special warfare" in South Vietnam, it has now gone on 12 long years. Regarding the war as having lasted 28 years, it is the longest war in modern history.

Viewed like this, it is no exaggeration to say that the war in Vietnam, in Indochina, has been a great battle of significance in world history, in terms of scope, the seriousness of its effects, and its duration. . . .

The Vietnamization of the War

One should have no illusions whatsoever concerning U.S. imperialism, represented by [President Richard] Nixon today.

As is well known, since the late U.S. President [Lyndon] Johnson agreed in March 1968 to convene the Paris talks on Vietnam, while partially suspending the bombing of the Democratic Republic of Vietnam, a "post-Vietnam argument" was brought forth on a great scale not only in Japan but throughout the world, spreading ideas as if "the Vietnam war has already been brought to an end". President Nixon, who replaced Johnson, while making full use of this propaganda, has continued and expanded the war of aggression in new forms, employing all kinds of even more ferocious and tricky methods.

The first policy of "Nixon's strategy" was the so-called "Vietnamization" of the war through the phased reduction of U.S. Forces then accounting for more than half a million men, to be replaced by a compulsory draft of one million Vietnamese, an increase in the Saigon puppet troops. Of course, this method is nothing new. During the Korean war, the then President [Dwight] Eisenhower, with Nixon himself as vice-president, put out the notorious slogan to "let Asians fight Asians". In his speech on the partial suspension of the bombing of North Vietnam, the then President Johnson suggested to go ahead with the increased reinforcement of the Saigon troops to cope with the growing fire-power of the enemy, obviously implying a "Vietnamization" program.

To Nixon himself, adoption of the "Vietnamization" program was becoming more and more unavoidable, as the U.S. expeditionary ground troops were already facing the imminent danger of collapse. . . . In this situation, Nixon, in an attempt to get out of the impending defeat, reduced the number of U.S. ground troops that had substantially been put out of action, and in their place, turned one million South Vietnamese into cannon-fodder to maintain the neo-colonialist rule. U.S. Ambassador to Saigon, [Ellsworth] Bunker paraphrased the true nature of the "Vietnamization" of the war when he said that it was meant to change the color of the corpses.

Vietnam Is Inundated with Bombs

The second point of "Nixon's strategy" was to put air power into action and intensify the bombing, exceeding by far the Johnson era. Of the bombs and shells totaling more than 15 million tons dropped in the 8 year period, from 1965 till the end of 1972, about 58% was used under the Nixon administration.

During the first 3 years after taking office, President Nixon escalated the chemical warfare even further. Some 1.88 million hectares of farmland was destroyed, and about 900,000 people of South Vietnam were poisoned. Poisoning by toxic chemicals has had genetic effects on the following generation, sharply increasing the birth rate of abnormal and deformed babies. In October 1970, a vast area in the northern part of South Vietnam was inundated with floodwaters, with tens of thousands of inhabitants falling victim to the disaster. One of the causes of this flooding was found to be defoliation operations carried out by the U.S. Forces.

> All-out efforts have been made to kill and wound as many people as possible by developing and using one 'sophisticated' new-type weapon of mass destruction after another.

Nixon's war of aggression in Indochina was escalated by the misuse of science and technology, as well. Since 1970, the U.S. Forces have been using super 7-ton bombs, every one being equal in destructive power to a small atom bomb, and which destroys all life within a square kilometer. All-out efforts have been made to kill and wound as many people as possible by developing and using one "sophisticated" new-type weapon of mass destruction after another. These include CBUs [cluster bombs], orange bombs, napalm, white phosphorus bombs, magnesium bombs, spider mines, perforation bombs, concussion bombs, defoliation bombs, nails or flechettes, dragon-tooth mines, magnetic bombs, guided missiles, etc.

Nixon's military men have perfected their so-called "electronic warfare". The U.S. Air Force [USAF] implanted a large number of small type transmission equipment units called "sensors" in the three countries of Indochina. These acoustic and seismic sensors can "detect" the sound and the slightest earth vibration not only of footsteps and vehicles but of every thing that moves, the messages of which would be instantly picked up by relay aircraft flying on constant missions. The signals would then be automatically transmitted to the USAF "Infiltration Surveillance Center" for computer analysis. Based on this data, U.S. bombers would take off immediately for bombing missions over the area. A kind of unmanned war, an automated war, has thus been developed. In this way, the U.S. Forces have tried to kill and wound people of Indochina at the minimum cost of their own lives and by the most "effective" means.

Nixon has continually ignored Johnson's statement on the total suspension of the bombing of North Vietnam. In May 1972, Nixon went so far as to mine Haiphong and other ports, harbors and rivers of North Vietnam for a total blockade, while intensifying the bombing and escalating the saturation bombing of the Democratic Republic of Vietnam on a greater scale than ever. In December 1972, Nixon trampled on the draft cease-fire agreement to which he himself had once agreed, and resumed the massive bombing and shelling of the Democratic Repub-

lic of Vietnam. Hanoi was exposed to carpet bombings by B-52s day and night. From December 18 through 28, 1972, taking the example of Hanoi alone, the U.S. Forces dropped 40,000 tons of bombs (equivalent to two Hiroshima-type bombs) on densely populated areas, killing and wounding about 2,500 of the civilian population.

Civilians lie dead after being killed by U.S. soldiers during the My Lai massacre. (Ronald L. Haeberle/Contributor/ Time & Life Pictures/ Getty Images.)

The U.S. Imperialists Are War Criminals

The third point of "Nixon's strategy" is the so-called "pacification program", the substance of which is nothing less than genocide. Genocide of the villagers of Song My [the My Lai massacre when around 500 unarmed Vietnamese citizens were killed] was committed under the Johnson administration, but those directly responsible for this genocide were actually found not guilty and acquitted. The troops under Nixon's command committed additional genocide in Balang An, Thanh Birth and other villages and hamlets (January–March 1969), turned a number of other villages and hamlets of South Vietnam into ruins, and killed all the inhabitants there. During the first three years of the Nixon administration, 3,000 hamlets of a total of 12,000 hamlets in South Vietnam were wiped out. In Quang Tri and Thua Thien provinces, for instance, 500 of the 870 hamlets, and in Quang Da province near Da Nang, 351 of the 441 hamlets were wiped off the face of the earth. Nixon has introduced large bulldozers into his "pacification program". A vast area of forests has been leveled, with the ecological cycle destroyed, depriving the farming population of their means of livelihood. . . .

> A vast area of forests has been leveled, with the ecological cycle destroyed, depriving the farming population of their means of livelihood.

"Nixon's strategy" as such has not been to achieve as great a result as he had intended. In particular, the counter-offensives launched at the end of March 1972 by the South Vietnam People's Liberation Armed Forces dealt heavy blows on the "Vietnamization" program, especially on the Saigon puppet troops, the core of this program. Nixon and U.S. imperialism were completely at a loss, unable to take any prompt effective action. Nixon grew more and more ferocious: on April 16, he ordered the bombing of Hanoi and Haiphong; on May 8, he issued another order to mine the territorial waters of North Vietnam to enforce a total blockade, and hit all targets with the greatest possible bombing and shelling. Toward the end of October 1972, Nixon expressed his readiness to sign the "peace accords", which shortly turned out to be a well-calculated gesture to help his re-election as President, and to cool off the struggle of the world peoples in solidarity with the Vietnamese people.

Agent Orange

Agent Orange was an herbicide used by the United States during the Vietnam War (1955–1975; U.S. involvement 1964–1975) to deprive Viet Cong and North Vietnamese soldiers of forest cover and food crops. "Operation Ranch Hand" was the code name for the application of Agent Orange, as well as other defoliants such as Agent White and Agent Blue, by specially equipped Air Force cargo planes. More than forty-six percent of South Vietnam's territory was sprayed with herbicide under Operation Ranch Hand between 1962 and 1970. Agent Orange proved to be the most effective of the herbicides, as it contained dioxin, an extremely toxic chemical agent. Within a few weeks after its application, Agent Orange would turn lush, green forests brown and barren. It also had a detrimental effect on humans.

In 1966, the North Vietnamese charged that herbicides such as Agent Orange were responsible for causing congenital deformities in infants. Three years later, a report in a South Vietnamese newspaper made the same allegation. That same year, a study by the National Institutes of Health presented evidence that the dioxin found in Agent Orange caused deformities in babies. The United States suspended the use of Agent Orange in 1970, and ended Operation Ranch Hand in 1971.

After the war, studies continued to probe the impact that the dioxin found in Agent Orange could have on people. Americans who served in South Vietnam and were exposed to Agent Orange reported high incidences of skin rashes, breathing problems, various types of cancer, and birth defects in their children. A class action suit brought by affected veterans against the Veterans Administration was settled out of court in 1985.

SOURCE. John A. Morello, "Agent Orange," Dictionary of American History. Ed. Stanley I. Kutler. 3rd ed. 10 vols. New York: Charles Scribner's Sons, 2003.

At the Paris talks which resumed early in December, however, Nixon had his representatives present unjust demands that trampled on the agreement already reached with the DRVN [Democratic Republic of Vietnam]. When these demands were rightly refused by the

DRVN and the PRG [Provisional Revolutionary Government of South Vietnam] of the Republic of South Vietnam, Nixon again resumed the total bombing and blockade of North Vietnam, trying to bring the people to their knees.

In the light of all these facts, it is crystal clear that the U.S. imperialists, headed by Nixon, are truly ferocious and tricky war criminals, who never hesitate at any inhuman and swindling action, with a mind of neither reason nor conscience.

The United States Lost the Battle for the Hearts and Minds of the Vietnamese

Nguyen Cao Ky

As the prime minister of South Vietnam from 1965 to 1967, Nguyen Cao Ky worked closely with U.S. diplomats, politicians, and military leaders in the fight to maintain independence from the North. In the following excerpt from his book *How We Lost the Vietnam War*, Ky blames the United States' inability to win the hearts and minds of the South Vietnamese, especially the peasants, as a chief factor in their defeat. The actions and policies of the United States ultimately drove a wedge between American soldiers and the Vietnamese citizens they were trying to protect. Ky maintains that U.S. forces failed to understand the Vietnamese and their way of life, trying instead to influence them through material gifts and aid. Additionally, he contends

---

SOURCE. Nguyen Cao Ky, *How We Lost the Vietnam War*. Lanham, MD: Stein and Day, 1978. Reproduced by permission.

that the relocation policies the U.S. forces imposed on peasants further divorced these individuals from their traditional way of life and actually offered them little protection.

Alongside the military war, fought with bombs and bullets, we had to fight another war—one to convince our own people that South Vietnam offered a way of life superior to that of the Communists. It was a war for the hearts and minds of the people.

America Misjudges the Vietnamese People

It was not, as some thought, a matter of simple materialism, a philosophy that started with filling bellies. [U.S.] Ambassador Ellsworth Bunker was hopelessly wrong when he told me on one occasion, "People are drifting toward Communism because they are poor. If you give the people everything they want—television sets, automobiles, and so on—none of them will go over to Communism."

Poor Bunker! He was trying to impose American standards of life on people he did not understand, people who basically had no desire for the so-called good things of the American way of life.

Like so many well-meaning Americans, Bunker, when he came to Vietnam, was unable to grasp the fact that he had made an excursion into a culture as different from America's as an African Negro's is different from that of an Eskimo. No man could hope to span the differences in American and Vietnamese culture and heritage in the short time of his appointment in our land. How could I explain to Bunker's Western mind, for example, that while an American would be lost with-

> Conscious of their dollar-bought superiority, the Americans patronized us at all levels.

out a future to conquer, a Vietnamese is lost without the refuge of the past.

"Material goods are not the answer," I replied. "It's much more important to win the hearts and minds of the people than to give them TV sets."

Bunker shook his head disbelievingly, and I felt, watching him, that he was wondering how this young upstart dared to utter such nonsense. But then Bunker no doubt believed in Napoleon's dictum that an army marches on its stomach, and saw no reason why civilians should be any different. But they were. . . .

The American Attitude Toward the Vietnamese Is Patronizing

The Americans controlled the fighting of the war. American aid financed the country; without it we could not survive. Americans selected or influenced the selection of our politicians and leaders, even at village level, and had a natural tendency to pick the most compliant rather than the most gifted. American culture—its films, television, and advertising—swamped our own.

Conscious of their dollar-bought superiority, the Americans patronized us at all levels. GIs thoughtlessly but hurtfully referred to Vietnamese as Dinks and Gooks, Slants and Slopes. (Charlie, Chuck, and Claude were reserved for the Viet Cong.)

Their contemptuous attitude was typified by an announcer on the American Forces Radio in 1970: "For those of you staying on in 'Nam, here's a little advice regarding our Vietnamese friends. As you know, they're kind of jumpy now, so please remember the golden rule. Never pat a Vietnamese on the head. Stand on low ground when you talk to them. They kind of resent looking up to you. Okay?"

Certainly the Vietnamese resented being patted on the head. The battle for the hearts and minds of the people was more fundamental to success even than air

U.S. Marines distribute ice cream at the Phu Thuong Orphanage. Such gestures failed to win the allegiances of the Vietnamese people. (U.S. Marine Corps/Stringer/Archive Photos/Getty Images.)

power or fire power. Yet someone, presumably a GI, painted in white letters on an old warehouse by the river in Saigon the legend: "Just grab the Gooks by the balls and their hearts and minds will follow."

Americans Institute Defensive Villages

Faced with these problems, the peasants of Vietnam became some of the war's most tragic casualties. All they asked for was the right to extract a living from the soil, as their forebears had done. Instead, millions became refugees, driven from their homes by either the Communists or, alas, the Americans. . . .

The Americans backed the idea [of relocating peasants to defensive villages to protect them from the Viet Cong] wholeheartedly, and by April 1963 Secretary of State Dean Rusk was claiming that "Already approximately seven million Vietnamese live in over five thousand strategic hamlets. The program calls for completion of another three thousand by the end of this year."

The truth is that only a relatively small percentage of them were viable. Some were situated in locations where defense was impossible and the Communists overran them. Some existed only on paper. They were never built because the peasants found that they could not get the relocation allowances they were promised and had to find the funds for creating fortified villages themselves.

Somehow, I had to make the scheme work. When I became prime minister I revived it under the name of "New Life Hamlets." But [former South Vietnam Prime Minister Ngo Dinh] Diem had replaced the original landlords with officials, while I decided to replace the officials with freely elected village chiefs.

The Americans were very helpful—in some ways too helpful, because my communities frequently became known as "American villages." It was inevitable, I suppose, when American troops moved in by helicopter exuding goodwill, and distributing bars of chocolate, portable battery-operated lavatories, toothbrushes, and the "Uncle Ben's" rice to a knot of wondering and silent men, women, and children who had never asked for anything more than to be left alone to grow their own rice. But this was something the American GI could not understand. He had been sent to a village and knew only that he had to give the villagers their "basic liberties," as outlined in the Pacification Program Handbook, so that

> Once the helicopter had whirred away, the chocolate, the comics, the portable lavatories were valueless against infiltrating Communists who slaughtered everyone who defied them.

he could report back, "The friendship of the villagers was secured and they are with us in this war."

But the "friendship" was as short-lived as the bar of chocolate. The villagers were not enemies, but once the helicopter had whirred away, the chocolate, the comics, the portable lavatories were valueless against infiltrating Communists who slaughtered everyone who defied them.

The United States Gives the Peasants Limited Options

[Overall U.S. Commander] General [William] Westmoreland decided that the only hope of containing Communist guerrilla forces was to have areas between New Life Hamlets which would be designated as free-fire zones after they had been cleared of Communists. Anything that moved in that area could be shot. "Until now the war has been characterized by a substantial majority of the population remaining neutral," Westmoreland warned. "In the past year we have seen an escalation to a higher level of intensity in the war. This will bring about a moment of decision for the peasant farmer. He will have to choose if he stays alive.

"Until now the peasant farmer has had three alternatives. He could stay put and follow his natural instinct to stay close to the land, living beside the graves of his ancestors. He could move into an area under government control, or he could join the VC. Now, if he stays put, there are additional dangers.

"The VC cannot patch up wounds. If the peasant becomes a refugee he does get shelter, food and security, job opportunities and is given a hope to possibly return to the land. The third alternative is life with the VC. The VC have not made good on their promises; they no longer secure areas. There are B52 bombings, the VC tax demands are increasing, they want more recruits at the point of a gun, forced labor to move supplies. The battle is being carried more and more to the enemy."

Fine words; but when I read the speech, I saw its true meaning instantly: the Americans had abandoned hope of winning the loyalty of the peasants. They had given in to the cadres of the NLF [National Liberation Front] and Viet Cong. And this meant an awful truth: from now on, there were to be no neutrals. Those who did not enter defensive villages or other government-controlled areas would have to suffer the consequences. Villages that went over to the Communists could—and would—be obliterated.

That almost standard, heartbreaking by-product of war emerged again. I saw it for myself. I remember taking up my helicopter one day, and suddenly seeing below me along a red road, under a blazing sun, a long snake of human beings winding its way endlessly. From where to where? There seemed to be millions of refugees, their pitiful belongings, their pots and pans and chickens carried on old men's backs, or jammed into baby carriages, old carts, or wheelbarrows. The line stretched from horizon to horizon, with here and there figures, perhaps left to die, littering the roadside as the slow-moving, almost Biblical caravan trudged toward a new life. Near the cities shanty towns sprang up overnight, homes made from gasoline cans or packing cases, hideous replicas of the poor but decent homes that had been drenched by the poison of men or burned with the fire of men.

> It was pointless for the Americans to promise better prospects for those who moved; they did not want better prospects.

The Continued Misunderstanding of the Vietnamese People

The Americans distributed aid generously, and tried to create job opportunities, but it was impossible to make them understand what was involved in transplanting

Vietnamese from one zone to another. Leaving aside the important aspect of ancestor worship and the dream of a perpetual family life, a Vietnamese village is a small, private world. Behind the bamboo hedge, ringed by rice fields, is a self-supporting world that has existed virtually unchanged for decades.

It was pointless for the Americans to promise better prospects for those who moved; they did not want better prospects. If the average villager amassed wealth it had to come from the land and that meant he was achieving his wealth at the expense of his neighbor. The Americans might earnestly believe that making money was the finest pursuit on earth. It was hard to explain to them that a villager who suddenly became rich was not so much respected as pointed at in shame.

North Vietnam Both Won and Lost the Vietnam War

Tai Sung An

Following the fall of Saigon to Communist forces in April 1975, the North Vietnamese proclaimed themselves victorious in the war for the reunification of their country and against the United States. In the viewpoint that follows, South Korean political scientist Tai Sung An argues, however, that when the damage and destruction to cities and villages across the country, as well as the enormous loss of life is tallied, it becomes more difficult to call the North Vietnamese accomplishments a victory. Their inability to rebuild after the war and lingering distrust between North and South has hampered progress, leaving many—including An—to wonder whether the reconstituted Vietnam will ever be as one. Tai Sung An taught at Washington College in Maryland until his death in 1998.

SOURCE. Tai Sung An, *The Vietnam War*. Cranbury, NJ: Farleigh Dickinson University Press, 1998. Copyright © 1998 by Fairleigh Dickinson University Press. All rights reserved. Reproduced by permission of the Associated University Press.

Nobody who writes about the Vietnam War can fail to note the terrible suffering that North Vietnamese communist expansionism and the American defense inflicted on the people of Vietnam, both North and South. The Vietnamese Communists' pride in their sacrifice and victory in the twentieth century will undoubtedly become a heroic chapter in the several millennia of Vietnamese history. As a rule, however, defeat in military conflicts costs dearly but so does the effort to achieve victory. Hanoi [the capital of North Vietnam] paid a very high price for its successful defiance of the world's greatest military and economic power, the United States, so as to make its victory dreadful in consequences, dubious in validity, and thus meaningless in significance. In other words, small nations such as North Vietnam must suffer terribly even in victory against a giant power, and the Vietnamese Communist victory was Pyrrhic [coming at too great a cost for the victor] at best.

The Expendable Forces of North Vietnam

The burdens borne by the Americans during the protracted, bloody Vietnam War were small compared with those of the Vietnamese. The war was marked by great brutality, and the Vietnamese Communists paid heavy costs for their cause. It is estimated that the total Vietnamese civilian and military casualties (both killed and wounded) on both sides made up about 10 percent of the entire population—more than 4 million. (That would be roughly proportionate to U.S. losses of 20 million.) According to [American political scientist] John E. Mueller's study, the Vietnamese Communist battle deaths during the Vietnam War were, "as a percentage of the prewar population, probably twice as high as those suffered by the fanatical, often suicidal Japanese during World War II." The Vietnamese Communists are, Mueller went on to

Photo on following page: North Vietnam succeeded in reuniting the country against the desire of the U.S., but the country also suffered greatly in the process, including the vast destruction of Hanoi. (Lee Lockwood/ Contributor/Time & Life Pictures/Getty Images.)

say, "virtually unique in the history of the last 160 years in their fanaticism and willingness to tolerate terrible heavy casualties."

In obsessive pursuit of victory, the DRV [Democratic Republic of Vietnam, or North Vietnam] leaders expended men the way the Americans expended munitions, thereby leading a generation of uninterrupted communist revolution to the borders of inhumanity. With the exception of nuclear weapons, nearly every piece of equipment in America's mighty arsenal was used in Vietnam. As General Fred Weyand said in 1976, "the American way of war is particularly violent, deadly and dreadful. We believe in using 'things'—artillery, bombs, massive firepower—in order to conserve our soldiers' lives." U.S. fliers dropped more than 7.5 million tons of bombs on Indochina—nearly three times the total tonnage dropped in World War II and Korea combined. The DRV regime revealed in December 1975 that the American bombing had destroyed virtually all industrial, transportation, and communications facilities built since 1954 and blotted out ten to fifteen years potential economic growth.

> American bombing had destroyed virtually all industrial, transportation, and communications facilities built since 1954 and blotted out ten to fifteen years potential economic growth.

Cataclysmic Damage Is Unleashed in Vietnam

La République Socialiste du Vietnam published in 1981 by *Éditions en Langues Étrangères* in Hanoi was very specific about the war damages of both North and South Vietnam. As far as the South was concerned, 9,000 out of 15,000 hamlets had been damaged or destroyed; 10 million hectares of farmland and 5 million hectares of forest lands affected; 1.5 million cattle killed; and the war had left behind 362,000 invalids, 1 million widows, and 800,000 orphans (including mixed-blood children abandoned by their American soldier fathers). As for the North, all 6 industrial cities had been damaged (3 of them razed to the ground); 28 out of 30 provincial capitals damaged (12 of them completely destroyed); 4,000 out of 5,788 communes damaged (300 completely destroyed); 1,600 hydraulic works, 6 railway lines, all roads, all bridges, and all sea and inland posts destroyed; all power stations seriously damaged; 5 million square meters of housing destroyed; 400,000 heads of cattle killed; and several hundred thousands hectares of farmland damaged.

At the time of the 27 January 1973 cease-fire, North Vietnam's cities lay in ruins, and their inhabitants were scattered throughout the countryside. Hanoi also suffered extensive disruption of its light industry—notably food processing (rice, sugar, fish, and tea) and textiles. The war also left behind the usual human wreckage—widows, orphans, and thousands of disabled veterans. According to a Senate Vietnam Subcommittee report, "at least one million persons became homeless." A former U.S. government official who was involved in the Vietnam War decisions and visited Vietnam with former secretary of defense Robert McNamara in June 1997 said: "There was an almost total absence of middle-aged men on the streets of Hanoi, men who would have been of fighting age during the war [and undoubtedly perished]."

> The war . . . was a tragedy of epic dimensions for the country and the people.

For the DRV regime, in short, the Second Indochina War was nothing short of cataclysmic. And whether the war was a valid adventure or a misguided endeavor for the Vietnamese Communist leaders, it was a tragedy of epic dimensions for the country and the people. One can and may ask: Where, in all the above sordid and tragic story, was the meaning of victory?

North Vietnam Outlasts the Enemy

The truth of the matter for the Vietnamese Communist side of the Second Indochina War was that the DRV leaders had never sought a real, clear-cut victory against the United States. What they had really attempted to accomplish was simply to outlast America politically, militarily, and psychologically with enormous casualties, destruction, and sacrifice—a sort of dubious or hollow victory. More to the point, the strategy of a protracted "people's war" worked both for and against Hanoi strategists. As a millennia-old Oriental philosophy says, each and every human act, as well as each and every human-made phenomenon, in the historical process is a two-way proposition in effect. The Hanoi leaders were well aware of the dangers of a protracted insurgency war, of the price such a war extracted from an already weary people, and of the difficulty of staying the course so long as the American side enjoyed the abundant material support and strength. To the battle-scarred DRV leaders, a blundering or Pyrrhic victory was definitely more to be valued than a humiliating defeat. A hollow victory, no matter how heroic in itself, usually tends to stand on thin ice and can easily turn sour. This is why the Second Indochina War was a drama without conclusive winners or genuinely victorious "heroes"—a Greek tragedy. . . .

Conditions in Vietnam Deteriorate Following the War

All historical periods and events are transitory without a final "happy or sad ending." Of course, this rule embraces a phenomenon known as war. Wars, unlike sporting events, are not over when they are over. "Even in defeat," as Carl von Clausewitz, a brilliant nineteenth-century Prussian military strategist, said, "the ultimate result is not always to be regarded as final." The outcome is "merely a transitory evil, for which a remedy may still be found in political and other conditions at some later date." The degree to which political and other conditions have changed since the end of the Second Indochina War is clearly manifest in Vietnam's postwar conditions, under which the Vietnamese Communists have lost more than they gained. In other words, Hanoi won the war and also lost it. This is, incidentally, why a communist victory in Vietnam did not turn out to be so a disaster for the United States in the post-Vietnam era. . . .

In his report for the CBS Television *Evening News* on 14 March 1985, [American television news reporter] Walter Cronkite stood on a street in Hanoi and called it "one of the world's most depressing capitals." He did not give postwar Vietnam a rave review. "The communist regime had failed miserably to put the nation's economy on anything like a valuable basis," Cronkite said. "It is a bicycle economy in a computer world." He called the public transportation system in Vietnam "decrepit," its agriculture "primitive," and its poverty "overwhelming."

The DRV regime in the second half of the 1970s had faced many problems and difficulties in proceeding with the task of integrating the "liberated South" into a single, uniform socialist society. The transformation of the South into the socialist model of the North had been far more difficult than the Hanoi regime ever expected, and the DRV leaders had found the South "ungovernable," or "unmanageable." The dour, brusque northerners and their freewheeling southern brothers may have been politically reunited, but they had remained deeply divided in spirit and attitude.

The Vietnam War Is a Parallel for the War in Afghanistan

Thomas H. Johnson and M. Chris Mason

Often considered the United States' most humiliating military exploit abroad, the Vietnam War is typically invoked as a comparison for U.S. involvement in a conflict on foreign soil that proves ultimately unwinnable. In the viewpoint that follows, Thomas H. Johnson and M. Chris Mason call upon this metaphor to evaluate the U.S. military engagement in Afghanistan that began in 2001. Johnson and Mason argue that there are many similarities between the Vietnam War and the War in Afghanistan and encompass not only commonalities between the landscape, enemy, and the United States' justification for participation, but stretch deeper to strategic failures, both military and political. The authors lament the inability of current U.S. policymakers to draw on the lessons of the Vietnam War when formulating policy on how to proceed in Afghanistan. Thomas H. Johnson is a professor and the director of the

SOURCE. Thomas H. Johnson and M. Chris Mason, "Saigon 2009: Afghanistan Is Today's Vietnam. No Question Mark Needed," *Foreign Policy*, August 20, 2009. Reproduced by permission.

program for culture and conflict studies (CCS) at the Naval Postgraduate School in Monterey, California. M. Chris Mason is a senior fellow at both the CCS and the Center for Advanced Defense Studies in Washington, D.C.

For those who say that comparing the current war in Afghanistan to the Vietnam War is taking things too far, here's a reality check: It's not taking things far enough. From the origins of these North-South conflicts to the role of insurgents and the pointlessness of this week's Afghan presidential elections, it's impossible to ignore the similarities between these wars. The places and faces may have changed but the enemy is old and familiar. The sooner the United States recognizes this, the sooner it can stop making the same mistakes in Afghanistan.

Similarities in Geography, Strategy, and Propaganda

Even at first glance the structural parallels alone are sobering. Both Vietnam and Afghanistan (prior to the U.S. engagement there) had surprisingly defeated a European power in a guerrilla war that lasted a decade, followed by a largely north-south civil war which lasted another decade. Insurgents in both countries enjoyed the advantage of a long, trackless, and uncloseable border and sanctuary beyond it, where they maintained absolute political control. Both were land wars in Asia with logistics lines more than 9,000 miles long and extremely harsh terrain with few roads, which nullified U.S. advantages in ground mobility and artillery. Other key contributing factors bear a striking resemblance: Almost exactly 80 percent of the population of both countries was rural, and literacy hovered around 10 percent.

In both countries, the United States sought to create an indigenous army modeled in its own image, based on

A U.S. marine searches an Afghan man in Mian Poshteh, Afghanistan, in 2009. (Joe Raedle/ Staff/ Getty Images News/Getty Images.)

U.S. army organization charts. With the ARVN [Army of the Republic of Vietnam] in South Vietnam and the ANA [Afghan National Army] in today's Afghanistan, assignment of personnel as combat advisors and mentors was the absolute lowest priority. And in both wars, the U.S. military grossly misled the American people about the size of the indigenous force over a protracted period. In Afghanistan, for example, the U.S. military touts 91,000 ANA soldiers as "trained and equipped," knowing full well that barely 39,000 are still in the ranks and present for duty.

The United States consistently and profoundly misunderstood the nature of the enemy it was fighting in each circumstance. In Vietnam, the United States insisted on fighting a war against communism, while the enemy was fighting a war of national reunification. In Afghanistan, the United States still insists on fighting a secular counterinsurgency, while the enemy is fighting a jihad [holy war]. The intersection of how insurgencies end and how jihads end is nil. It's hard to defeat an enemy you don't understand, and in Afghanistan, as in Vietnam, this fight is being played out in a different war.

> It's hard to defeat an enemy you don't understand, and in Afghanistan, as in Vietnam, this fight is being played out in a different war.

U.S. Military Failures in Vietnam and Afghanistan

This is but the tip of the iceberg of a long list of remarkable parallels. What's really startling are the deeper strategic connections. The United States lost the war in Vietnam, historical revisionism notwithstanding, because of a fatal nexus of political and military failure, and the exact same thing is happening in Afghanistan. As [U.S. defense policy analyst] Andrew Krepinevich noted many years ago, the army failed in Vietnam because it insisted on fighting a war of maneuver to "find, fix, and destroy" the enemy (with what became known as "search and destroy missions") instead of protecting the people in the villages. Today these tactics are called "sweep and clear missions," but they are in essence the same thing—clearing tiny patches of ground for short periods in a big country in hopes of killing enough enemy to make him quit. But its manpower pool was not North Vietnam's Achilles heel and neither is it the Taliban's. Almost exactly the same percentage of personnel in Afghanistan has rural reconstruction as its primary mission (the

Provincial Reconstruction Teams) as had "pacification" (today's "nation-building") as their primary mission in Vietnam, about 4 percent. The other 96 percent is engaged in chasing illiterate teenage boys with guns around the countryside, exactly what the enemy wants us to do.

The Problem of Government Legitimacy

Meanwhile the political failure in Kabul is Saigon *déjà vu*. A government that is seen as legitimate by 85 or 90 percent of the population is considered the *sine qua non* [essential element] of success by counterinsurgency experts. After the Diem Coup [during which Ngo Dinh Diem, the president of the Republic of Vietnam, or South Vietnam, was ousted from power by ARVN generals and assassinated after the United States pledged not to interfere], this was never possible in Vietnam, as one incompetent and utterly corrupt government succeeded another. None was legitimate in the eyes of the people. Contemporary descriptions of the various Saigon governments read almost exactly like descriptions of the Karzai government today. Notwithstanding all the fanfare over this week's [August 2009] presidential voting in Afghanistan, the Kabul government will never be legitimate either, because democracy is not a source of legitimacy of governance in Afghanistan and it never has been. Legitimacy in Afghanistan over the last thousand years has come exclusively from dynastic and religious sources. The fatal blunder of the United States in eliminating a ceremonial Afghan monarchy was Afghanistan's Diem Coup: afterwards, there was little possibility of establishing a legitimate, secular national government.

It doesn't matter who wins the August elections for president in Afghanistan: he will be illegitimate *because* he is elected. We have apparently learned nothing from Vietnam.

The War in Afghanistan Is Not Like the Vietnam War

David Miliband

While comparisons between the Vietnam War and the War in Afghanistan, which began in 2001, have been often uttered to support arguments that the Afghan conflict is unwinnable, David Miliband refutes these comparisons in the following viewpoint. Miliband argues that there are many differences between the two conflicts, including distinctions between the impetus for going to war, the enemy being fought, and the opportunity for the United States to build a strong and resilient democracy. Miliband believes that these differences make the War in Afghanistan a war worth fighting and one that the coalition of forces led by the United States is capable of winning. David Miliband is British Labour politician and Member of Parliament.

SOURCE. David Miliband, "The Danger Is Being Outgoverned, Rather than Outgunned," *New Statesman*, vol. 139, January 25, 2010, p. 25. Copyright © 2010 New Statesman, Ltd. Reproduced by permission.

The deaths of two British soldiers on 15 January [2010] and the attacks on government buildings in Kabul [the capital of Afghanistan] three days later were a reminder of the challenges of the campaign in Afghanistan. Last year, the *NS* [*New Statesman*] warned that Afghanistan risked becoming another Vietnam, with western forces bogged down in an unwinnable war and waning popular support at home. I take the warning seriously. But I don't accept the thesis.

A Direct Attack and an Unpopular Enemy

The conflict in Vietnam was the product of a world divided by the cold war. The UK and its European partners did not join the US in Vietnam, unconvinced by the arguments for intervention. By contrast, the intervention in Afghanistan was triggered by a direct attack against the US on 11 September 2001. It has commanded widespread global support since then and the rationale for our continuing effort remains a direct concern about the threat to our national security if Afghanistan once again becomes safe ground for al-Qaeda under the umbrella of the Taliban.

The Vietcong were a broad, deeply rooted, popular movement tapping into nationalist feelings throughout the country and society, and their appeal and legitimacy ultimately proved superior to that of the South Vietnamese regime. The Taliban have limited appeal due to their ethnicity, geography and the recent memory of their brutal, reactionary misrule. Afghans fear their return. They worry that when coalition troops begin to leave, the Afghan government will be too weak to stand up to the Taliban. That is why international troops are focusing on building up the Afghan army. It is now 100,000-strong, on the road to 134,000 in the course of this year. General McChrystal [U.S. commander of the International Security Assistance Force and U.S. forces in Afghanistan]

is getting international forces not just to train Afghans, but to fight alongside them—there is no quicker or better way to build the expertise of the army than learning side-by-side in theatre.

Legitimizing the Democratic Afghan Government

To remain resistant to Taliban intimidation, Afghans need to know that their government can provide basic justice and maintain order. This is especially relevant as the Taliban seek to offer an alternative to the state. They appoint their own shadow governors and administer

Unlike the Vietcong, the Afghan insurgency is disorganized and disunified, thereby leaving an opening for a democratically elected government such as that of Hamid Karzai (right) to gain legitimacy. (**Shah Marai/AFP/Getty Images.**)

AMERICANS BELIEVE THE WAR IN AFGHANISTAN HAS BECOME LIKE THE VIETNAM WAR

CNN conducted a telephone poll of Americans October 16–18, 2009, to determine whether or not they believed the war in Afghanistan was becoming like the Vietnam War. The sampling error is +/- 3 percentage points.

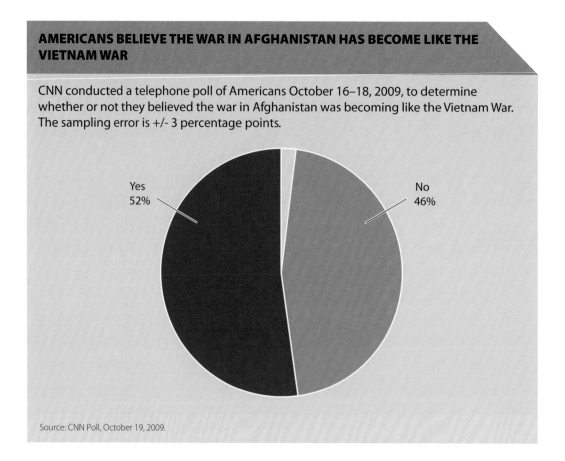

Yes 52%

No 46%

Source: CNN Poll, October 19, 2009.

their own crude brand of "justice". The danger is that, rather than being outgunned, the Afghan government is outgoverned. So it must build on and implement President [Hamid] Karzai's promise to tackle corruption. Provincial and district governors need to be given more power to govern and reach out to communities. That will include working with shuras [councils] of local elders to resolve disputes and expand social and economic provision.

One example, in Helmand, is Governor Gulab Mangal's wheat distribution programme, supported by the UK, which has helped more than 35,000 farmers to grow wheat for the open market instead of opium poppies, the profits from which fill the Taliban coffers.

The enemy we face in Afghanistan is a diffuse network of insurgent groups with diverse motivations. The Taliban leadership is linked to al-Qaeda. The great mass of fighters is not. Most are driven by pride or the pursuit of profit or power rather

> Where the Vietcong were unified, the insurgency [in Afghanistan] is a coalition of convenience that is capable of being divided.

than ideology. Where the Vietcong were unified, the insurgency is a coalition of convenience that is capable of being divided. In his inauguration speech, President Karzai committed to an open and inclusive settlement for Afghanistan, beginning with a peace jirga—a gathering of the leaders of tribes and groups that make up Afghan society. We must support the government in its efforts to draw conservative Pashtun nationalists away from the insurgency. We must separate those who are prepared to participate in the free and open society enshrined in the Afghan constitution from the hardline ideologues whom we must face on the battlefield.

Keys to Victory in Afghanistan

Neighbouring countries are suffering from the terrorism, drugs and crime that spill over Afghanistan's borders. As a result, it is becoming increasingly clear within the region that a stable, sovereign Afghan state is in the interest of all its neighbours. We need to build trust between these countries about each other's intentions. Pakistan is key. The history of finger-pointing (at best) with its neighbour has been replaced by co-operation. The Pakistani army's offensive in the Federally Administered Tribal Areas means that the Taliban are being squeezed on both sides of the border.

The implications for how we succeed are clear: military and development resources are critical, but they need to be channelled towards a clear political strategy aimed at maintaining the support of the Afghan people, dividing the insurgency and building regional co-operation. That is the task when more than 70 countries and international organisations meet in London on 28 January to discuss Afghanistan. We will be looking to President Karzai's government to show that its intentions on security and governance will be carried through into action. And the international community must renew and redouble its commitment to success.

This is a critical year for Afghanistan. The tempo of operations will increase—so, too, the resources. We are not trying to build a colony for ourselves. We are trying to prevent it becoming a crucible once again for attacks against the rest of the world. This is a necessary and achievable goal.

CHAPTER 3

Personal Narratives

A North Vietnamese Man Describes His Decision to Join the Army

Nguyen Van Hoang, as told by David Chartoff and Doan Van Toai

Photo on previous page: Young Vietnamese children stand in the bombed-out remains of the provincial capitol building in Xuan Loc, site of the last major battle of the Vietnam War. **(Dirck Halstead/ Contributor/Time & Life Pictures/Getty Images.)**

The son of a Workers' Party member who served in the Ministry of Cultural Affairs in Hanoi, Nguyen Van Hoang was not destined from his birth to join the National Liberation Front and fight to unify Vietnam. He was a painter in the tradition of his family and a teacher. However, after a U.S. bomb killed his fiancée, he was compelled to join the army to avenge her death. In the following viewpoint, Hoang recounts the events leading up to his enlistment in the army and describes his family's opposition to his actions. His uncle, an official within the party, pleaded with him not to go because it would be a useless sacrifice. Looking back on his enlistment, he admits that, had he known the Communist Party's boasts of grand victories were lies, he would not have gone to war.

SOURCE. Nguyen Van Hoang, as told by David Chanoff and Doan Van Toai, *Portrait of the Enemy*. Copyright © 1986 by David Chanoff and Doan Van Toai. Used by permission of Random House, Inc.

My Grandfather was a Confucian scholar, a Mandarin at the Imperial Court in Hue. Because he was anti-French, he decided to quit his government position and retire to a little farm in Ha Dong. With his few acres of paddy land, he kept himself busy farming and disassociated himself entirely from politics and from the French authorities. My father joined the Workers' Party and became deputy secretary of the Ha Dong Party branch. Later he was assigned to the Ministry of Cultural Affairs and transferred to Hanoi, where I grew up.

When I was in school my mother wanted me to do my advanced studies in electromechanics. She was sure that hydroelectricity would be developed in the North and that I could have a good career in that field. My father had different ideas about it. Painting was a tradition in our family, and he wanted me to continue it. He's got a strong will, and in the end I enrolled at the Institute of Arts and Trades. When I graduated I became a teacher.

The Desire for Revenge Drives a Young Man to War

Generally speaking, not all of the artists in North Vietnam follow the regime wholeheartedly. For an artist like myself, nothing is more beautiful than the ability to live your life freely. And there's not much appealing about the Communist regime in that regard. But I volunteered for the army anyway because of a personal tragedy. During one of the air strikes in Haiphong, my fiancée was killed by an American bomb. Immediately afterwards I decided that I had to go South to fight. At the time—this was in the summer of 1967—I thought that the Liberation Army was riding the crest of a wave. If I didn't join up right away I'd miss my chance to take revenge. I reasoned that the Americans must be bombing the North in retaliation for their defeat in the South. I thought the NLF [National Liberation Front] was on the verge of winning the decisive battle and that they would take Saigon in the very near future. I desperately wanted to go and kill a couple of Americans to relieve the bitterness I felt.

When my family learned that I had volunteered they were very unhappy about it. My mother cried for several days and nights straight. My father didn't cry, but he was obviously in distress. The day I left, my mother told me that both of them had been up the entire night, and that my father had been weeping along with her. When I said goodbye, my father told me, "You have to look after yourself, son, and try to return safely. For myself, I'm just trying to think of this as a study trip abroad for you. But be careful. Try to follow discipline and not get punished. And don't be too daring in the fighting. Don't make yourself a useless sacrifice. You are an educated man. It's not your vocation to be a soldier. That's a career that anyone can follow who knows how to pull a trigger. I'm unhappy that you're going. I want to see you back again."

> Many people were volunteering, without any idea of what kind of hardship and violence they were letting themselves in for.

Personally, I didn't think it was going to be that dangerous. In general, most of the people in the North were very confident at that period. Many people were volunteering, without any idea of what kind of hardship and violence they were letting themselves in for. As far as I was concerned, I trusted the government and believed what they were saying. I really thought the revolution was near victory.

The North Vietnamese Recruit Soldiers to Sacrifice in Battle

My father and my uncles saw it differently. One of my uncles was Hoang Tan Linh, the deputy chief of the Central Cadres Organizing Office in Hanoi. When he heard that I had volunteered he said, "Why are you joining? Don't you know the war in the South is a colossal sacrifice of troops? They're sending soldiers to the South to be killed at a merciless rate. They've taken most of the young men from Hanoi and from all over already, and they'll keep taking them. In war there has to be death. But this war isn't like when I fought against the French. Now the losses are in the thousands and tens of thousands. If you go now there's only one fate—unbearable hardship and possibly death—a meaningless death."

This uncle was a ranking cadre and he always said that in the end we would win. But he stressed to me that this was a period when the sacrifice of troops was necessary. The government was intent on fighting hard and violently, and they needed massive manpower. He said the destruction that was going on was savage and frightening beyond what I could imagine. [For a period of time before 1967, Nguyen Chi Thanh, the overall military commander in the South, followed a strategy of direct confrontation with American and ARVN (Army of the Republic of Vietnam) forces. Liberation Army casualties were enormous.] That was what he meant by a "colossal sacrifice."

But even if I had understood that, I still would have gone. In my family I was considered a very strong-willed person, like my father. Once my mind was made up, there was no budging me. I wasn't happy about joining the army. In fact, during my basic training I used to slip home every two or three days because I was so homesick. But I was absolutely determined to go South—that was irreversible.

But I'll tell you, had I realized that everything we were hearing about victory was nothing more than a big bluff, I never would have left.

A Young Man Explains His Decision to Resist the U.S. Draft

Malcolm Dundas, as told by Alice Lynd

In the 1960s, American men were still subject to compulsory military service, or the draft. As the Vietnam War dragged on into the late 1960s, many young men who were being drafted to fight became apprehensive about the possibility of dying in a war that they did not believe in. To protest the draft, some men burned their draft cards; others left the United States to live in Canada so as not to have to fight. Malcolm Dundas decided instead to stay and fight the draft. He became a conscientious objector (CO), someone who officially opposes the war on moral or religious grounds, and refused to participate in any activities to aid the war effort. As a result, he was sentenced to eighteen months in jail. In the following account of the time leading up to his decision to become a CO and the subsequent prison sentence, Dundas reaffirms his decision to oppose the war and resist the draft, even from the confines of prison.

SOURCE. Malcolm Dundas, as told by Alice Lynd, *We Won't Go: Personal Accounts of War Objectors*. Copyright © 1968 by Alice Lynd. Reprinted by permission of Beacon Press, Boston.

The decision to refuse is not something, for me, that is so concrete, so solid, that it never changes. . . . It evolves, revolves, grows, changes form and stature. The draft seems so overpowering—places one in such a helpless position that it is very hard to tell another person what to do. The hardest thing about resisting is that you just do not win (in the legal/political sense). Morally, perhaps, but, still, the draft goes on. Jail or exile does not stop wars directly. It gives a strong voice to dissent and to personal courage. It is not a question one can answer once and for all time—yet, in the terms of the law, one our age must!

My resistance to the draft is mostly a personal stand. It has ramifications outside myself—but the choice to resist, and the avenues, are personal. That is the nitty-gritty of the whole question. When the banners are gone, it is you, personally, who must face exile or prison.

I think the greatest stumbling block to one's becoming free to act is fear. Fear of an unknown and seemingly harsh path. I grew up with no knowledge of the CO [conscientious objector] position. People with such ideas did not exist in the Central Valley of California. In these formative years, I had only my brother, books, and animals as companions. I guess the mystique of the farm and rural life was a great factor in my subsequent attitude towards people and later wars. I played some war games, but, when school began, I was never involved in the usual wrangles of kids my age. Their quarrels and battles seemed so useless and silly. It is hard to say from here what experiences (like these) were the shapers and pushers. I was always an "outsider." . . .

Becoming a Conscientious Objector

The actual act of resistance took several steps. I was classified as a conscientious objector. Then I faced a choice of limited alternative service or noncooperation. I requested a hearing. At that hearing, I presented a two-page statement of noncooperation (March 5, 1966). While there, I attempted to return my draft cards to the board—they refused to accept them. I then signed a document stating that I would not do any form of alternative service. On April 15, 1966, I received an order to report for alternative service—dated for April 20, 1966. I returned that order and explained that I felt myself no longer under their jurisdiction—that I could not possibly accept their orders. In August of 1966, I was visited by two FBI agents. They informed me of their mission and my rights. I agreed to answer their questions. . . . They asked me if I would cooperate and I reiterated that I didn't feel I could cooperate with an illegal and immoral law. On December 9, 1966, I received a letter requesting that I appear for arraignment on December 12, 1966, in Sacramento Federal Court. I appeared, acting as my own defense counsel. The case was transferred to San Francisco, on my request. [*Trial date was April 29, 1967, and on May 17, 1967, an eighteen-month sentence was pronounced.*]

> When I first took out the CO papers, I was, I felt at the time, doing the most radical, sincere act I could.

When I first took out the CO papers, I was, I felt at the time, doing the most radical, sincere act I could. When I received the I-O [objector] status with no appeals, I relaxed again. No thunder bolts or such had torn my life apart—I was no different, outwardly at least. I still had a respect for laws. I felt that the law itself was the law of the land and therefore someone should obey it. But I began to see what it was doing to people in the South, and in Africa, and throughout this country, and I began to know that it had to be abolished, that you can't make a slave system more equitable. You have to abolish it and start with something where all people are free. I was romantically and intellectually ready for prison, if my beliefs were not received with concern and justice.

I have fluctuated many times and still do. My position has changed somewhat—I am more anarchist than radical—more love-oriented than political. . . . After years of a scoffing agnosticism, I have broadened my personal witness to the forces of Love/God everywhere. . . .

Arguments Against Forced Participation in the War

Legally, I am attacking the Selective Service Act on constitutional grounds. Namely, the Thirteenth Amendment, which prohibits involuntary servitude. To back it up I am using the United Nations Charter and the Declaration of Human Rights; the Army Field Manual; the Nürnberg Tribunal decisions; the London Treaty; the Geneva Convention of 1954; and the Kellogg-Briand Pact. The latter treaties support the struggle against this war in particular. They are useful in providing evidence that the war is illegal, genocidal, etc. After that I will attempt to prove that by complying with Selective Service, one becomes a party to the crimes of genocide and illegality of the war. Unfortunately, it is pretty clear that I will not be able to bring this evidence in testimony. . . . You are faced with the court saying, well, you broke a law and that is the only thing that is relevant; . . . the Vietnamese war itself is a political question and therefore not arguable in court.

> I want people to question their too ready acceptance of atrocity and government edicts as their law.

So the only arguments left are those of moral persuasion. I want people to question their too ready acceptance of atrocity and government edicts as their law. I want people to think about the record of lies and evidence of deception that is this war in particular and all wars in general. Then I want them to question themselves as to their role in the making of war or living off the death and destruction of others for a profit. I want to reach people—as a person, not as a case number. If my case gave one other person the courage to be then a revolution would have been accomplished. . . .

Fighting Through the Doubt

The greatest pressure I feel is doubt. The dull, pounding, nagging feeling of doubt. The helpless feeling one has when faced with the magnitude of wars and a government's power. The feeling of not being able to gauge one's actions to the scale of the war and all its ramifications. It is horrible to realize that your voice, your protest, doesn't stop people from killing and being killed. People want so much to see the effect of their actions, and for the noncooperator that is not possible. The war, the grossness of the way of life based on war, keeps me in my position of opposition to any such acts by the government. I guess I feel as [socialist Eugene] Debs did, or St. Francis, that one's place is always with those who are not free or are not filled. It is the mark of a human being: the need for *love*; the ability to be not one of the poor or enslaved, but to feel responsible, to evoke concern on the part of others, to be a witness to one's faith in love or humanity or God—that is the pressure that keeps one going on. . . .

> I am not hateful of the government—'pity' is more the word. They are trapped too—impotent to do anything beyond the execution of laws and rules.

Advice to Those Considering Positions of Resistance

. . . What can I say to one going the same route, or contemplating such a route. Politically it's a good move—for the movement—but when all the speeches are over it is you who must do the time or fight to avoid doing time.

Read all you can about what others have done—question others about their stands—but, sift it all through your perception of what is right and wrong for *you*. You will never fully be sure, but you should be as aware of all the ramifications of your actions as you can be. When you have done this, then make the choice. If you find then that you can't stick to it, then drop out of the action—don't place an unwanted burden on your life out of a sense of duty or such—your life is your life and not a movement's.

I guess that my case is just that, my case. A record of what I have done in one aspect of my life. A record of an act of faith and, I trust, love. I am not hateful of the government—"pity" is more the word. They are trapped too—impotent to do anything beyond the execution of laws and rules. In short, they are not free to be alive. The years of power and "liberalism" are telling on them. Rhetoric is failing them and now brute force replaces dialogue. Somehow we must reach them—behind the fist is still a man and he can be reached and his ideas changed. He need not agree with you, but he should be aware that you have as much a right to believe, free of repression, as he does—it is a mutual liberation. I hope, then, that my words may reach some people—help them, give them a chance to be. . . .

Reflections from Jail

Aug 31, 1967: Is it worth the price? Given the choices, yes; but one can't really do a comparative. My life is my communication—the prison is the unaware, unloving world of systems and hatred.

It's a martyrdom because most people are afraid—either of the time spent or social ambitiousness lost through stigma.

Given the reality of no real freedoms I encase my body/soul because I feel I am freer than the unaware blind fearful man in the outside plastic world. I choose this "slavery" because others attempt to coerce my life.

An American Woman Justifies Her Protest of the Vietnam War

Ethel Taylor

As a middle-class, middle-aged American woman, Ethel Taylor never imagined herself to be the type that stirred up trouble. However, as a result of her opposition to the Vietnam War, she caused enough trouble to land herself in jail on multiple occasions. In the excerpt from a 1990 interview in the following viewpoint, Taylor describes her unsanctioned trip to North Vietnam, her protest activities at home, and the consequences of these actions, including alienation and arrest. Still, she saw herself as a true patriot—a person with the duty to question the government instead of blindly following whatever it proclaims. Ethel Taylor was a member and co-founder of Women Strike for Peace, an organization founded to enact a ban against nuclear testing and to help protest and end the Vietnam War.

SOURCE. Ethel Taylor, "Ethel Taylor," *The Loyal Opposition: Americans in North Vietnam, 1965–1972*. Edited by James W. Clinton. University Press of Colorado, 1995, pp. 148–164. Reproduced by permission.

Late December of 1969, [I traveled to Vietnam along with] Cora Weiss of New York and Madeline Duckles of Berkeley. [I paid for the trip] personally. We were invited by the North Vietnam Women's Union to discuss the setting up of a clearinghouse, the Committee of Liaison With Families of Servicemen Detained in Vietnam, in this country for the transmission of mail and packages from prisoners of war and their families and vice versa. This was because the Vietnamese did not abide by the Geneva Convention on prisoners because they said this was not a declared war [and that] the United States, by bombing them without provocation, was committing a criminal act. So the POWs [prisoners of war] were not even called prisoners of war by the Vietnamese; they were called war criminals.

I guess this was the most significant thing that I have ever been involved in, to be part of this plan which would notify parents, wives, and children that their sons, husbands, and fathers were still alive or were not alive. Before I went, word got around to the prisoners' families that I was going. I received hundreds of letters from families asking if their kin were alive because they didn't know. There was very little information from Vietnam about whether they were or not. When I went in '69, there were families who hadn't heard from their sons since '64, when they knew they were shot down.

Soldiers Believed the Peace Movement Lengthened the War

There was a family out in my area who contacted me because their son was shot down in 1964. This family was really instrumental in notifying all the families in the area and also as far as California that I was going. And I came back with thirty-six letters. It almost sounds like a television situation. I came back at Christmas with these letters for families who had no idea whether their sons were alive or dead. And I was able to call them and tell them that their sons were alive and that I had letters from them which I was putting in the mail right away. [This was their first indication that their kin were alive.] I received wonderful letters from them. Of course, there were all these other families who had sent letters for me to take to Hanoi, but I had no information for them. But it was really a unique experience to be able to do this, and Cora, Madeline, and I really felt specially blessed to be able to do this.

> I say now and I said then that the administrations lengthened the war, and the peace movement tried to stop it.

The family that lived in my neighborhood whose son was shot down in 1964 didn't know if he was dead or alive. In addition to thirty-five other letters, I was able to bring back a letter to them from their son. They were so thrilled and grateful that they promised when their son came back they would have a big party and their son and I would stand together receiving guests. It never happened! When their son came back, he would have nothing to do with me because he was convinced that the peace movement lengthened the war. He wrote a letter to the local newspaper expressing that view, and I responded with a letter to the editor debunking that position. I wrote that the POWs, due to their imprisonment over all those years, had no idea what the feelings of the American people were and how sentiment changed to an antiwar position as the war dragged on.

[Their son] felt the peace movement's activities lengthened the war. He didn't know that during the presidential campaign of 1964, Lyndon Johnson was quoted as saying on August 12, 1964:

> Some others are eager to enlarge the conflict. They call upon us to supply American boys to do the job that Asian boys should do. They ask us to take reckless action which might risk the lives of millions and engulf

much of Asia and threaten the peace of the entire world. Moreover, such action would offer no solution at all to the real problem of Vietnam.

Despite [making] this statement, upon winning the presidency, Johnson immediately sent fifty thousand more young men to Vietnam. [Richard] Nixon became president, claiming he had a plan to end the war, and four years later, with fifty thousand American soldiers dead, the war ended on the same terms that could have ended it four years before. I say now and I said then that the administrations lengthened the war, and the peace movement tried to stop it. . . .

Fear Alienates Americans from Each Other

I was amazed that I was such a hot item to the service clubs when I came back from Vietnam. The first to invite me, an Optimist Club, was very cordial. It became known to other clubs that I gave interesting talks on Vietnam. I received invitations from Lions, Rotaries, etc. There were frightening incidents, like being hit over the head with a heavy stick while demonstrating outside "Re-elect Nixon" headquarters. But the worst kind of experience was when people were afraid to talk to me because they were fearful that their peers would think they were soft on communism.

My last speaking engagement to clubs was devastating. When I started to speak, men in the back started to shout and scream, "Hanoi Hannah." It was taken up by practically everyone; it was an experience I was to have on other occasions. In the audience were a priest, a prominent businessman, and someone I knew slightly. As I left, I met them outside, and they apologized for the behavior of the group. I asked them why they didn't defend me on the inside, and they admitted that they didn't want to incur the wrath of the Rotarians. I wrote to the program director who had invited me and said how saddened I was that Father so-and-so and the others were afraid to defend me. He sent back a scathing letter in which he said he had questioned them, and they denied talking to me outside.

> The government had been successful in their anti-communist zeal to put fear into people and to alienate one group of citizens from another.

Another time, I was invited to speak at a church to commemorate World Peace Day. I didn't know anything about the church, but when I arrived and met the minister, he informed me that I was in [anti-communist] John Birch territory. The chairwoman announced that after I spoke, she would escort me to the back of the room, and I would receive people who wanted to speak to me. I started to speak, and, as if by signal, one row after another stood up and walked out, just like at a funeral. I kept on speaking, and when I was through, protocol prevailed, and the chairwoman escorted me through the empty church to the back of the room. No one was there.

I started to leave, and a woman dashed out of the women's room, put a piece of paper in my hand, and dashed out. When I got into my car, I read it. It said, "My name is so-and-so; my phone number is so-and-so. I want to know more about Women Strike for Peace, but I was afraid to ask you in front of the people." This was what was more frightening than any other kind of abuse. The government had been successful in their anti-communist zeal to put fear into people and to alienate one group of citizens from another.

A Middle-Aged Woman Stands Up for Her Beliefs

[My trip to Vietnam] was the most meaningful experience of my life, besides having children. I had been in the peace movement for a long time and was exceedingly

committed to the cause of peace and justice. But this experience was beyond that. We carried our opposition to the war to the land our government called "enemy," and we found friends. Our ability to make connections between POWs and their families was an extra bonus.

That this trip and my other activities might be considered treason by proponents of the war did not concern me. I was sure that right was on our side. I only learned later, through my FBI files, that there was continuous consultation between a federal attorney in Philadelphia and the FBI about whether I should be tried for sedition because of my open support of draft resisters. After two years of such correspondence, the case was dropped.

The Women Strike for Peace group demonstrates against the escalation of the war in Vietnam in 1966. (AP Images.)

[My opposition to the war] was certainly a learning experience for me about myself. I was a middle-aged, middle-class American woman who thought I would live out my whole life without seeing the inside of a jail as a prisoner, and there I was, locked up two times. At the time, it seemed easier to get arrested than not get arrested . . . to do things that were a little drastic than not to do them. There were so many times where it was absolutely essential that I put my body where my mouth had been. Going to Vietnam was a natural sequence because it was important to have credibility. It was important for me to go to Vietnam to see for myself and to meet all these people myself, to see what they were thinking, and see what the devastation was. And I did.

Arrests and Mistreatment

I remember one instance. At that time, women were wearing hats and gloves, white gloves. And even if we weren't active in Women Strike for Peace, we would have worn them because that was the style. But wearing hats and white gloves was a political statement because it encouraged women who saw us on television or saw pictures of us in the newspapers to look at us and say, "They're just like me. They're not wild-haired radicals." They identified with us.

> Trusting a government without asking questions is a dangerous thing to do. A patriot asks questions.

There I was in my hat and my gloves in the paddy wagon. We arrived at the jail, and the back door opened. I was first. I looked down. There was about a five-foot jump with no steps. I stood there in my hat and white gloves, waiting for the policeman to come and help me down. And I waited. The policeman came and said, "Jump, sister." So I knew my life had changed and was on another track. And that was what we did. We seemed to put aside fear. My basic philosophy was,

"What can they do, hang me? Electrocute me? What can they do to prevent me from defending what I believed to be the right thing?" And it wasn't terrible; it was just unusual. One thing led to another.

[I was arrested] twice. [Each time, I stayed in jail] overnight. Something that happened in the second arrest is and has always been a mystery to me. The arrest was the result of the Capitol sit-in. The next morning, we appeared before a judge for arraignment, and he set a date for trial later in the summer. As we were leaving, a federal marshal stopped about six of us, including myself, and took us into a ladies' room and handcuffed us to a pole and left us there. A few hours later [without explanation], we were released.

The Difficulty of Being a Patriot

I think I did as much as I could do. I could do all that I did because I had the full support of my husband and children. I'm sure there are things I could have done more effectively, but I don't think I could have been any more involved than I was without being a basket case.

It's not easy to be a patriot. It's not just Fourth of July, fireworks, and the American flag. It's not including a statement against abortion in the Pledge of Allegiance, which is being considered in some areas. Being a patriot sometimes can mean being very unpopular because sometimes you have to go against what is conceived by most people as being patriotic. Patriotism is being against the policy of your government when you think the government is wrong. No "my government, right or wrong" for a patriot. I think that I and all of the people who acted and demonstrated against the war in Vietnam were the patriots. Trusting a government without asking questions is a dangerous thing to do. A patriot asks questions.

I think that if [the American people] had immediately understood the genesis of the war in Vietnam, they would have immediately opposed it, but by the time people realized what was going on and where Vietnam was, we were totally committed. They didn't know the history of Vietnam, a country which had fought off invaders for more years than we have been a nation. They didn't know that we financed eighty percent of the French Indochinese War, and when the French were beaten, we stepped in. It has always seemed incomprehensible to me that we destroyed a country ten thousand miles away, killed untold numbers of Vietnamese, caused the deaths of fifty-eight thousand Americans and who knows how many wounded and scarred in an effort to eradicate communism. . . .

The Symbol of a Flawed Government

Vietnam, to me, is a symbol of flawed government; I'm talking about our government. So my anger and indignation is still directed at Vietnam-thinking which goes on, even as we speak. The Vietnam War was a war not only against the Vietnamese but also a war against the American people. That war is not over. It's the war that keeps on giving. Thousands and thousands of Vietnam veterans are ill, mentally and physically, because of that war. Agent Orange may be responsible for illnesses in their children. It's like the atom bomb dropped upon Hiroshima [at the end of World War II], the fallout from which is still affecting the third generation of Japanese. Vietnam was like bacteriological warfare. It infected all of us. I just hope that there won't be a post-Saudi Arabian syndrome and then a post-somewhere else syndrome. The lesson of Vietnam has not been learned, and that's what prevents much mellowed feelings on my part.

A U.S. Pilot Relates His Experiences as a Prisoner of War

Richard Bates, interviewed by Vera Clyburn

Richard Bates was a rear-seat weapons systems officer on a F-4 fighter bomber during the Vietnam War. In October 1972, Bates and his pilot were shot down in enemy airspace but survived to be captured. They were marched north to Hanoi, where they were imprisoned. In the viewpoint that follows, Bates is interviewed by Vera Clyburn of the Library of Congress and describes how he suffered interrogation, starvation, and torture at the hands of his captors. He recalls practicing mind games to keep sane during the ordeal and how the American POWs (prisoners of war) used early-release prisoners to get information about the names and numbers of POWs in North Vietnam back to the authorities at home. Sometime in late March 1973, Bates was released as part of the Paris Peace Accords that signaled the end of the war.

SOURCE. Richard Bates, interviewed by Vera Clyburn, "Interview with Richard Bates," *Experiencing War: Stories from the Veterans History Project*, American Folklife Center, Library of Congress, May 28, 2005. Reproduced by permission of the author.

Richard Bates: I spent the first six months flying combat operations and in six months I flew about 135 combat missions, somewhere around 400 hours of flying. I . . . very quickly got into a special mission that was called a fast fax, or forward air control. Typically the forward air control mission is done by like assessment type airplanes in South Vietnam where there were troops on the ground that you coordinated with and there were battles happening. The forward air controller talked to a guy on the ground, and he said essentially here is where the good guys are, here is where the bad guys are.

And then he would coordinate the fighter bombers to come and drop their bombs. In North Vietnam, first of all, the atmosphere was too dangerous for the small airplanes to fly, number one. Number two, . . . theoretically there were no, you know, good guys; we had no troops on the ground. So we took that concept of forward air control and we used the fighters in force and a few of us would spend essentially all day up flying.

Not necessarily dropping anything but looking for . . . where the surface-to-air missile sites were and the guns and the trucks that were transporting the supplies to the south, and then we would have the fighters come in and control the strike. A more typical combat mission lasted anywhere from an hour to two hours. We were generally in the air about six. So I did that mission, . . . that was my main mission over there. We also, among the squadron that I was attached to . . . happened to be the first squadron in the Air Force in the world that dropped laser-guided bombs.

We dropped laser-guided bombs, the things so-called smart bombs that you hear about on the news. I think we were the first ones in the world to be dropping them operationally. Sometimes that gets a little bit lost. The people don't remember that. I did that for about . . . six months. On the 5th of October of 1972, I was on a 4 air control mission and my airplane was shot down. Myself and the pilot in front were both forced to eject. We were both captured and taken as prisoners of war. That was the first day of my six-month crash diet.

Shot Down and Captured

Vera Clyburn: Do you remember much about that time or care to share any of that time when you were captive? What was it like? How did you handle the stress of being captured?

Richard Bates: Oh, yeah. The shock of the shoot down itself is enough that sort of puts into, I would say, a little bit of a time war. We were in the area that was, you know, obviously highly populated and I was captured essentially immediately. I was in the southern part of North Vietnam about 350 miles or so I think from Hanoi, which is where their main capital was in the north, where all of the POWs ended up. So I spent the next two months there on the ground in a bunker or traveling on the way to Hanoi. It didn't take two months of travel, but initially they just kept me right on the ground.

> I was in the southern part of North Vietnam about 350 miles or so I think from Hanoi [when my plane was shot down].

And finally, we started moving north . . . both by truck and on foot and . . . at that time I was reunited with my pilot; he and I were together. . . . He sustained two broken legs in the ejection, of the small bone in your lower leg, fibula I believe, the small bone. So he was having a little bit of a trouble with the walking. But . . . we stopped about two-thirds of the way in an area we think was near the city of Thanwaw and were kept for another week or two without moving and finally were put into a truck and spent all night and half the next day traveling into Hanoi, until we reached the prison that everybody calls the Hanoi Hilton. From there it was another 30 days or so of solitary and an initial interrogation. And . . . there was physical abuse.

> I . . . suffered some physical abuse when I got to Hanoi that was mostly just beatings and getting struck with rifle butts and that sort of thing.

I don't know that I can't very well say . . . that I suffered what would be considered torture as some of the guys who were there for a year for every month I was there. The first day I was captured in the southern part of the country, I did get my arms, my elbows roped up and pulled back behind my back until my elbows touched, which dislocated my shoulders. I spent about four hours like that. So you know, and I also suffered some physical abuse when I got to Hanoi that was mostly just beatings and getting struck with rifle butts and that sort of thing.

Staying Mentally Alert

Vera Clyburn: Was there anything that helped you get through that time? Sometimes people have had like their tokens, flag on their face or whatever to help them to endure a period of captivity.

Richard Bates: . . . I say you found out very quickly if you were religious or not. I remember . . . [I] initially would recite the Lord's Prayer. . . . Very quickly I changed from the Lord's Prayer to the 23rd Psalm because the part about the valley of the shadow of death seemed to be very meaningful. You did some mind games. Throughout my captivity . . . I tried to break my day up into periods of physical activity, mental activity and then rest. I . . . say my arms when they were tied up, my arms were pretty useless when they untied me. So I was initially just trying to get my motion, some strength in my arms. One of the things I started doing for the mental activities [was] I started thinking back on my life, and the different things, and I tried to mind game. I tried to memorize all of the states. So I memorized the 50 states and I alphabetized them.

And then I tried to recall all of the capitals, so . . . I did the capitals in the alphabetical order that I remembered the states. And then I alphabetized the capitals and set the capitals in alphabetical order. Then I did the states in alphabetical order of the capitals. I see South Carolina and West Virginia were wrong, which really makes me mad now. Those are the only two mistakes I made. Then I tried to start remembering some times of my youth and I graduated with a high school class of I think about 96. I was able to . . . recall all of the names of 94 of my high school graduating class. There were two that I never got. And that didn't happen like overnight. . . . You either got 10 or 15 immediately. Then you get five or six more.

What was really amazing to me was, . . . your mind is really an amazing machine I guess. Because you would have your mental periods and you were doing things and you do your exercises, then you are in your rest period. And you would be laying there just not thinking particularly about anything. Then all of a sudden some event or some name would float up from your subconscious, and it was as if someone walked up beside you and touched you on your shoulder and said, You remember this? Wow! I eventually moved on to people I knew in college, and the list got to be, you know, at 1500 I quit.

> I lost 60 pounds in six months, which ought to answer the food question.

Vera Clyburn: Do you remember anything about the situation in terms [of] did you have enough food, were there supplies enough for the need at the camp at the time?

Richard Bates: Just a minute. (Pause.) I lost 60 pounds in six months, which ought to answer the food question.

I should go back now. I need to lose about a hundred. But maybe another 60 would be all right. But not . . . adequate medical treatment of any kind. Food was just barely enough to sustain life. The food that they fed us in the prison in Hanoi was food they wouldn't eat themselves. So . . . , essentially they had one answer to medical problems, and it was a white tablet, which we were pretty sure it was a sulpha tablet . . . That was their answer to everything. Many of us had dysentery. . . .

Getting Information Out of North Vietnam

Vera Clyburn: In some of the wars sometimes people would have international organizations coming in to check on the prisoners. [There was] nothing of that sort?

Richard Bates: No, no, sir. The International Red Cross, before I was a prisoner, had been there once or twice. What they were allowed to see was extremely controlled. Extremely controlled. They were not allowed anywhere near where we were. Once again, within the last 30 days before I was released we all did receive Red Cross packages, but that was, you know, the last 30 days.

Vera Clyburn: Within that time I'm sure you met a lot of people and sometimes they talk about people who were able to leave and bring back in information as such. Were there any times that you were able to get information out to comrades?

Richard Bates: We had I believe . . . a total of seven early releases. Six of those were absolutely dishonorable as far as we were concerned. Our code essentially said I'll accept no treatment that's better than my fellow prisoner. Going home was better treatment. So six of those guys went home pretty much against orders. I realize that may sound very harsh, but that's the way it was. We had one prisoner who was—again, this is a funny story if you think about it in some ways. He was a Navy seaman from South Dakota which is where I'm from. And he went through his boot camp in San Diego and then he was assigned to a cruiser that was on station off the Gulf, right in the Gulf there, just off, in Hanoi and Bien Hoa.

He had been in the Navy a grand total of ninety days I think, maybe a hundred and twenty days. I believe he worked in the mail room. One night the guns were going, the ships guns were going to shell harbor, and one of the other sailors had gone up and seen that it was really wild, you know, it's like fireworks. So Doug went up on deck to watch the guns shooting and had a concussion from the gun shooting and he fell overboard. He floated in the water all night and washed up in the high water, and the next morning he was captured and taken as prisoner of war. He was a young farm kid, 18 years old, not particularly worldly, glasses, you know.

> Our code essentially said I'll accept no treatment that's better than my fellow prisoner. Going home was better treatment.

And the Vietnamese almost didn't know what to do with him. He got involved in the prisoner of war system. He without too much trouble convinced them that he was A, harmless and B, stupid. And since he was an enlisted guy, he was made to do a little bit more menial things, some manual labor type management things, sweeping. . . . One day he was sweeping, and this is how little attention they paid to him. One day he was in the courtyard of the Hanoi Hilton we called Heart Break Hotel, he was sweeping and sweeping and sweeping, and . . . pretty soon he was sweeping at the front door, and he's sweeping, and now he's standing in the streets of Hanoi; he's escaped.

And so there he was. He said here I am in my striped pajamas, a half a foot taller than everybody else. Even though I'm short, what do I do, what's my plan and where do I go. So he just kind of went back in. He was actually, they wanted to send him home because he was no good to them, to the Vietnamese in their eyes as, you know, propaganda wise.

Vera Clyburn: Getting information that they could retrieve?

Richard Bates: They were going to send him home and he wasn't going to go, but he was ordered to go home because he was considered by us really a non-combatant type fellow. When he came home he brought the names of about 375 . . . POWs, and other very valuable information. The names of prisoners, other prisoners, particularly prisoners who had not previously been known . . . were POWs. I'm not saying that the other early releases did not bring back information that was useful to us. I'm just saying that their circumstances were different and they shouldn't have gone. But Doug was, Doug had brought back an awful lot of information.

Release from Camp

Vera Clyburn: I see. Do you remember the date your release came?

Richard Bates: Oh, yes.

Vera Clyburn: Could you share a little of that with us?

Richard Bates: . . . Part of the protocols of the Peace Accord, of course, was that . . . we had to be told and given pieces of paper that showed what the release terms were. I think within six or seven days of the signature of the protocol. So we were all put into an auditorium and they gave us this and passed these pieces of paper out. We went back and the release provisions were—they gave it three ways. You could be released, one camp, then the next camp and then the next camp or essentially . . . the first person captured was the first person released. The Vietnamese sort of did it both ways. They realigned the camps a little bit or brought someone or moved a few people around so they did in fact [or] in essence both of those things. I was in a camp which was called the zoo at the time and on the 28th—on the 27th of March of '73, the Vietnamese had told us that there was going to be a release and half of the camp was going to be released.

I was in the second half, not the first half. But there were some political snags that happened on that day and so the release didn't happen. It's interesting the Vietnamese felt all of a sudden that they had lost face, because they told us that there was going to be a release and there wasn't. And so they didn't say anything more to us about release after that. Although the release that was supposed to happen on the 27th happened on the 28th. And that night as I was being locked into my cell, the guard that was doing the lockup kind of looked at us and said, you know, tomorrow perhaps, maybe if things go smoothly, you go home, you know. And the next morning we got up and our cells were unlocked.

. . . Each building . . . also had a courtyard with the high wall around it. And one of the things I did, I was an observer to communicate between groups. I got out the door and looked through; there's a crack that you could see in the main compound of the camp. And I went out and looked, I came back and went to the senior ranking officer and I said I think something is going to happen today. He said why. I said because I think I just saw [newscaster] Walter Cronkite walking across the field there, [across] the dirt. In fact, it was him. They had oh, a week or two before they—at one point in time they took you to a room that had a bunch of clothes, pants and shirts. You tried on

> " I think I just saw Walter Cronkite walking across the field there. "

pants and shirts until you found something that fit you, then they wrote down what the size was and that's what they released us in, just a pair of like dickies and shirt, buttoned shirt.

They also . . . , you know, they spent a lot of time, at least made a token effort in the last 30 to 60 days to show, you know, how nice they had been to us, sent a little gym bag with some of their soap and cigarettes and your tin cup that you went with. We had gotten these packages and some of the guys had gotten things from home. Very, very few, but about a week before we were released we were told to take the things that we wanted to go home with and that we didn't necessarily need between now and the time we went home and put them in a certain area and . . . what they did was they scrutinized those things just to make sure that there wasn't what they considered contraband going out.

I had such a poor reputation with the guards that when I got my stuff to go home, they had pretty much thrown everything away. So I got nothing back from that. But then one morning the release came, and they said take everything that you are going home with and leave it outside your room, and they locked the doors . . . so that we couldn't go back in. They then took us over to the head, we called the head shed, the main part of the camp, and we went in these rooms and we found the bags with our names on it, and we put our clothes on. I was worried about shoes because I have got such big feet; they didn't have shoes anywhere near big enough for me. Everybody else had shoes, you know, . . . but me and although they did have a pair of shoes that I was able to get on and leave with. Then . . . we got on a bus and drove to the airport. . . .

A Vietnamese, one of our interrogators, called our names out, and then we stepped forward and reported to an American officer and were handed off to another American who walked us out to the back of the airplane, we got on the airplane. And, of course, it was typical, you know, everybody held their breath until the airplane was airborne. Then it was a pretty good cheer that went up, but the real cheer went up when the captain came on the intercom and said that we had flown out of Vietnamese air space.

CHRONOLOGY

1884   June 6: The Treaty of Hue or Protectorate Treaty establishes French colonial rule in Vietnam.

1885–1889   The Can Vuong movement attempts, unsuccessfully, to rid Vietnam of its French colonizers and establish an independent Vietnam.

1930   February 3: Ho Chi Minh and other Vietnamese exiles living in China found the Communist Party of Vietnam.

February 10: In the Yen Bai mutiny, Vietnamese soldiers, with the aid of civilian members of the Viet Nam Quoc Dan Dang (VNQDD, the Vietnamese Nationalist Party), stage an uprising against the French colonial army. The uprising fails.

1941   May 19: The Viet Minh common front is founded to oppose and expel French colonial rule. When Japan occupies the country during World War II, the Viet Minh fight them with aid from the United States and China.

1945   September 2: Ho Chi Minh declares the Democratic Republic of Vietnam (DRV) an independent state after the Japanese surrender to the Allies.

1946   June: In an attempt to retain control over Vietnam, France declares the southern third of the country to be the "Autonomous Republic of Cochinchina." The nationalists in the north respond by adopting the first Constitution of the Republic, triggering French reoccupation of Hanoi and igniting the Franco-Viet Minh War, also known as the First Indochina War, which will last for the next eight years. The United States supports France to counter Communist China and the Soviet Union's support of Ho Chi Minh and the DRV.

1954   March 13–May 7: The Viet Minh win the Battle of Dien Bien Phu, ending French military action in Vietnam.

April 26–July 21: France and Vietnam meet with representatives from the United States, China, the Soviet Union, and other nations at the Geneva Conference. Per the conference agreement, the country is divided into north and south zones at the seventeenth parallel to be governed, respectively, by the Viet Minh and the State of Vietnam, and elections are scheduled for July 1956 to reunify the country. The conference also produces three ceasefire accords, one each for Cambodia, Laos, and Vietnam, ending the First Indochina War.

July: Ngo Dinh Diem is appointed prime minister of South Vietnam under Emperor Bao Dai. His "Denounce the Communists" campaign results in the arrest, imprisonment, torture, or execution of tens of thousands of suspected Communists in South Vietnam.

1955   June: Diem cancels the upcoming 1956 reunification elections.

October 26: Three days after winning rigged elections, Diem declares himself president of the Republic of Vietnam. While the U.S. government has opposed many of Diem's authoritarian actions, they continue to support him and the Republic because he is anti-Communist.

1956   After the French leave Vietnam, the U.S. Military
        Assistance Advisor Group (MAAG) begins training
        South Vietnamese forces.

1957   Communists in South Vietnam undertake a campaign
        of low-level insurgency in response to Diem's totalitar-
        ian rule. Ho advises them to use minimal violence,
        promote the movement as nationalistic instead of
        Communist, and avoid alienating peasants from the
        movement by explaining any violence to them. More
        than four hundred South Vietnamese officials are killed.

1959   January: North Vietnam authorizes increased military
        action by Communists in South Vietnam. Large-scale
        offenses against the South Vietnamese army commence;
        weapons and personnel travel to the south from the
        north along the Ho Chi Minh Trail, which will become
        one of the main targets of military action as the war
        continues.

        July 8: Army Major Dale Richard Buis and Master
        Sergeant Chester Melvin Ovnand, members of the U.S.
        MAAG, are killed in an attack by Communist forces in
        South Vietnam. They are the first Americans to die in
        the Vietnam War.

1960   The National Liberation Front is officially formed in
        South Vietnam to oppose the government of Diem.
        Diem labels them the Viet Cong.

        November 8: John F. Kennedy is elected president of the
        United States.

1961   With the aid of U.S. advisors, Diem implements the
        Strategic Hamlet Plan and begins relocating peasants
        from their homes to defensible villages to isolate them
        from the influence of Communists. The program fails

to solidify support for the Diem government and actually increases peasant sympathies for the Communists.

1962   The U.S. military begins using the herbicide Agent Orange to defoliate the dense jungle where the Viet Cong hide and to destroy their crops and food supply. The use of this chemical would result in the death of hundreds of thousands of Vietnamese and cause birth defects in half a million Vietnamese.

1963   January 2: The Viet Cong defeat South Vietnamese and U.S. forces in the Battle of Ap Bac. It is the first major victory for the Viet Cong.

        June 11: Thich Quang Duc self-immolates (burns himself to death) at an intersection in Saigon in protest of Diem's harsh policies against Buddhists.

        November 2: South Vietnamese generals overthrow President Diem and execute him and his brother. Individuals within the U.S. government are aware the coup will take place and pledge not to intervene nor punish the generals for their actions. Political instability grips South Vietnam.

        November 22: President Kennedy is assassinated; Vice President Lyndon B. Johnson takes the high office.

1964   August 2–4: The Gulf of Tonkin Incident: The USS *Maddox*, a destroyer, alleges fire from North Vietnamese Navy torpedo boats. A second naval battle ensues on August 4, but no evidence of North Vietnamese engagement is ever found.

        August 7: The U.S. Congress passes the Gulf of Tonkin Resolution authorizing President Johnson to employ conventional military force in South Vietnam without a formal declaration of war. U.S. involvement in the war escalates.

1965 March 2: Operation Rolling Thunder commences with the intense bombing of targets in North Vietnam. The campaign continues throughout the following three years of the war and results in severe damage to North Vietnam.

March 8: The U.S. ground war in Vietnam begins with the deployment of 3,500 Marines to South Vietnam.

May 21–23: The Vietnam Day Committee organizes the largest teach-in protesting the Vietnam War at the University of California, Berkeley. Reports estimate that between 10,000 and 30,000 people attend.

December: The number of U.S. troops in South Vietnam surpasses 200,000.

1966 Protests in the United States against the war increase with one hundred veterans attempting to return their medals to the White House. Worldwide opposition to the war grows.

1967 January 8: The largest ground force operation in Vietnam, Operation Cedar Falls, begins. Viet Cong tunnel complexes and supplies are found and destroyed; however, the operation is not deemed a victory.

January 14: U.S. citizens' opposition to the war broadens as 20,000 to 30,000 people participate in a Human Be-In protest in San Francisco.

March 25: Rev. Martin Luther King, Jr. speaks out against the Vietnam War and leads an antiwar march in New York City.

October: Thousands of draftees return their draft cards during Stop the Draft week. A demonstration with around 100,000 protestors occurs at the Lincoln Memorial in Washington, D.C.

1968 January 30: The Tet Offensive begins as Communist forces begin attacking military and civilian control centers across South Vietnam with the goal of inciting the South Vietnamese to rise up and overthrow the government. The U.S. and South Vietnamese forces eventually defeat the Viet Cong forces while inflicting many casualties, but U.S. public opposition to the war increases.

January 30–March 3: During the Battle of Hue, North Vietnamese forces execute more than 5,000 civilians and bury them in mass graves found by the U.S. and South Vietnamese forces when they eventually drive the North Vietnamese out of the city. The city is destroyed during the fight.

March 16: U.S. soldiers kill hundreds of unarmed Vietnamese civilians, mostly women, children, and elderly in the My Lai and My Khe hamlets. News of the My Lai massacre is withheld from the American public.

November 5: Richard Nixon is elected president of the United States. He promises to end the Vietnam War and bring peace to the region.

1969 January 28: President Nixon and his advisors agree on a plan of Vietnamization, which will involve the withdrawal of the more than 500,000 U.S. troops from Vietnam and turn control of the war and fighting over to the South Vietnamese army.

March 18–26: With Operation Menu, U.S. forces begin bombing Cambodia in an attempt to disrupt the supply flow and training camps of North Vietnamese forces in the country. The American public is not informed of the bombing campaign, because Cambodia had maintained neutrality throughout the Vietnam War, even though they tolerated Viet Cong presence in their country, to avoid being drawn into the war at large. The bombing of a neutral country could be considered a war crime and would have ignited even greater protest against the war from U.S. citizens.

September 2: Ho Chi Minh dies of heart failure in his home.

November 12: With independent investigative journalist Seymour Hersh's report of the My Lai massacre, the U.S. public finally learns of the incident. Antiwar sentiments in the United States erupt, and even those who previously had been indifferent about the war begin to openly oppose it.

1970   May 4: At Kent State University in Ohio, National Guardsmen open fire on unarmed students protesting the war. Four protesters are killed and another nine are wounded. The shootings ignite a series of nonviolent and violent protests across the country and antiwar sentiments continue to solidify.

August 4: Secret negotiations between U.S. national security advisor Henry Kissinger and North Vietnamese politician Le Duc Tho begin in an attempt to end the war.

1971   June 13: The *New York Times* begins publishing excerpts from the Pentagon Papers, a study commissioned by U.S. secretary of defense Robert S. McNamara in 1967. The report, officially titled *United States-Vietnam Relations, 1945–1967: A Study Prepared by the*

Department of Defense, chronicles U.S. political and military activity in Vietnam. Its publication reveals government deception throughout that time period, with politicians often not telling the American public the real reason for the country's continued engagement in the region.

1972   During the presidential election, Nixon reduces the number of troops in Vietnam by 70,000 in response to criticism from his Democratic opponent, George McGovern, that he is not doing enough to halt U.S. participation in the war.

October 8: Kissinger and Tho announce that an agreement has been reached regarding the conditions necessary to end the war. However, South Vietnam president Nguyen Van Thieu, who was unaware that the talks were even taking place, opposes the agreement.

November 7: Richard Nixon is elected to a second term as president.

1973   January 27: The Democratic Republic of Vietnam (North), the Republic of Vietnam (South), and the United States sign the Agreement on Ending the War and Restoring Peace in Vietnam as part of the Paris Peace Accords. The agreement calls for a ceasefire; however, fighting continues on a smaller scale between the North and South as the American troop withdrawal commences.

December 10: Henry Kissinger and Le Duc Tho are jointly awarded the Nobel Peace Prize. Tho declines the award stating that there is still no peace in his country.

The U.S. military draft is ended.

1974   January 4: President Thieu announces the resumption
        of the war and claims the Paris Peace Accords void.

        August 9: In light of the revelations of the Watergate
        Hearings, President Nixon resigns and Gerald Ford
        takes his place.

        December 13: The final North Vietnamese offensive,
        the Ho Chi Minh Campaign, begins. North Vietnamese
        forces attack the Phuoc Long Province in South
        Vietnam. When the capital city falls on January 6, 1975,
        and the United States does not intervene, the North is
        emboldened to continue its push to overtake Saigon.

1975   April 21: In the face of intense political pressure,
        President Thieu resigns. In his final speech, he accuses
        the United States of being "inhumane," "not trustwor-
        thy," and "irresponsible."

        April 30: After two days of intense fighting in
        and around Saigon, the Vietnam War comes to a
        close as South Vietnamese forces surrender and a
        North Vietnamese tank runs through the gates of
        Independence Palace. During the final days of the
        war, U.S. personnel and civilians, as well as South
        Vietnamese citizens who are at risk if they remain in
        the city, are evacuated.

FOR FURTHER READING

Books

Ang Cheng Guan, *The Vietnam War from the Other Side: The Vietnamese Communists' Perspective*. London: Routledge, 2002.

Michael R. Belknap, *The Vietnam War on Trial: The My Lai Massacre and the Court-Martial of Lieutenant Calley*. Lawrence, KS: University Press of Kansas, 2002.

James F. Dunnigan and Albert A. Nofi, *Dirty Little Secrets of the Vietnam War*. New York: Thomas Dunne Books, 1999.

Van Nguyen Duong, *The Tragedy of the Vietnam War: A South Vietnamese Officer's Analysis*. Jefferson, NC: McFarland & Co., 2008.

Sylvia Ellis, *Britain, America, and the Vietnam War*. Westport, CT: Praeger, 2004.

Ilya V. Gaiduk, *The Soviet Union and the Vietnam War*. Chicago: I.R. Dee, 1996.

Marc Jason Gilbert, *The Vietnam War on Campus: Other Voices, More Distant Drums*. Westport, CT: Praeger, 2001.

Herman Graham III, *The Brothers' Vietnam War: Black Power, Manhood, and the Military Experience*. Gainesville, FL: University Press of Florida, 2003.

Patrick Hagopian, *The Vietnam War in American Memory: Veterans, Memorials, and the Politics of Healing*. Amherst, MA: University of Massachusetts Press, 2009.

Michael P. Hamilton, *The Vietnam War: Christian Perspectives*. Grand Rapids, MI: Eerdmans, 1967.

George C. Herring, *The Secret Diplomacy of the Vietnam War: Negotiating the Volumes of the Pentagon Papers*. Austin: University of Texas Press, 1983.

Okinori Kaya, *What I Think of the Vietnam War*. Tokyo: Japan National Foreign Affairs Foundation, 1968.

Henry Kissinger, *Ending the Vietnam War: A History of America's Involvement in and Extrication from the Vietnam War*. New York: Simon & Schuster, 2003.

John Norton Moore and Robert F. Turner, *The Real Lessons of the Vietnam War: Reflections Twenty-five Years after the Fall of Saigon*. Durham, NC: Carolina Academic Press, 2002.

Jonathan Neale, *A People's History of the Vietnam War*. New York: New Press, 2003.

Caroline Page, *U.S. Official Propaganda During the Vietnam War, 1965–1973: The Limits of Persuasion*. New York: Leicester University Press, 1996.

Pham Kim Ving, *In Their Defense: U.S. Soldiers in the Vietnam War*. Pheonix, AZ: Sphinx, 1985.

John Prados, *The Hidden History of the Vietnam War*. Chicago: I.R. Dee, 1995.

Roberto Rabel, *New Zealand and the Vietnam War*. Auckland, N.Z.: Auckland University Press, 2005.

Hemen Ray, *China's Vietnam War*. New Dehli: Radiant, 1983.

Mary Susannah Robbins, *Against the Vietnam War: Writings by Activists*. Syracuse, NY: Syracuse University Press, 1999.

John Carlos Rowe and Richard Berg, eds., *The Vietnam War and American Culture*. New York: Columbia University Press, 1991.

William Schoenl, *New Perspectives on the Vietnam War: Our Allies' Views*. Lanham, MD: University Press of America, 2002.

Anthony Short, *The Origins of the Vietnam War*. New York: Longman, 1989.

R.B. Smith, *An International History of the Vietnam War*. New York: St. Martin's Press, 1983.

Bruce O. Solheim, *The Vietnam War Era: A Personal Journey*. Westport, CT: Praeger, 2006.

Cao Van Vien and Dong Van Khuyen, *Reflections on the Vietnam War*. Washington, DC: U.S. Army Center of Military History, 1980.

Karen Zeinert, *The Valiant Women of the Vietnam War*. Brookfield, CT: Millibrook Press, 2000.

Periodicals

Stewart Alsop, "Why We Can Win in Vietnam," *Saturday Evening Post*, June 4, 1966.

Stephen T. Banko, III, "Let's Start the Stream of Psychic Healing," *Vital Speeches of the Day*, December 2009.

Christopher Buckley, "Good Morning, Hanoi," *Forbes*, May 24, 2010.

Geoffrey Cain and Joshua Kurlantzick, "Agent of Influence," *Washington Monthly*, January-February 2010.

John Gange, "The Mix of Fact and Myth," *Nation*, August 24, 1964.

Jeffrey Goodman, "How to Be Patriotic and Live with Yourself," *Atlantic*, February 1966.

Medhi Hasan, "Obama Is Wrong: This Is His Vietnam," *New Statesman*, December 21, 2009.

Edward G. Lansdale, "Viet Nam: Do We Understand Revolution?" *Foreign Affairs*, October 1964.

Jerry Lembcke, "The Times, They Changed," *Chronicle of Higher Education*, April 30, 2010.

Harold H. Martin, "Fighting an Unseen Enemy," *Saturday Evening Post*, November 24, 1962.

John McCain, "John McCain, Prisoner of War: A First-Person Account," *U.S. News & World Report*, May 14, 1973.

Robert J. McMahon, "The Politics and Geopolitics of American Troop Withdrawals from Vietnam, 1968–1972," *Diplomatic History*, June 2010.

Kim Nguyen, "'Without the Luxury of Historical Amnesia': The Model Postwar Immigrant Remembering the Vietnam War

Through Anticommunist Protests," *Journal of Communication and Inquiry*, April 2010.

Richard E. Rubenstein, "We're Unfair to Draft-Card Burners," *Saturday Evening Post*, February 12, 1966.

Yoshikazu Sakamoto, "The Japanese and Vietnam," *New Republic*, September 4, 1965.

Jean-Paul Sartre, "Why I Will Not Go to the United States," *Nation*, April 19, 1965.

Melvin Small, "Bring the Boys Home Now! Antiwar Activism and Withdrawal from Vietnam—and Iraq," *Diplomatic History*, June 2010.

William L. Stearman, "Lessons Learned from Vietnam," *Military Review*, March-April 2010.

Vu Van Thai, "A Regional Solution for Viet Nam," *Foreign Affairs*, January 1968.

Tai Tovy, "Peasants and Revolutionary Movements: The Viet-Cong as a Case Study," *War in History*, April 2010.

Nick Turse, "The Pentagon Book Club," *Nation*, May 17, 2010.

Websites

Battlefield: Vietnam (www.pbs.org/battlefieldvietnam). On this PBS website, visitors can read a brief history of the Vietnam War, explore the chronology of events leading up to and occurring during the war, and learn more about the Viet Cong's guerrilla warfare and the U.S. air war. The site also provides detailed information about the Siege of Khe Sanh and links to additional PBS websites dedicated to Vietnam War topics.

Explorations, The Vietnam War as History (www.digitalhistory.uh.edu/learning_history/vietnam/vietnam_menu.cfm). This site, part of the Digital History website produced by the University of Houston, provides a topical overview of the Vietnam War divided by issues such as "The Decision to Escalate," "The Anti-War Movement," and "Lessons of Vietnam." Each tabbed topic includes links to additional, primary source documents presenting a range of views from individuals on both sides of the war.

Learn About Vietnam (www.vietnamembassy-usa.org/ learn_about_vietnam). The Embassy of the Socialist Republic of Vietnam in the United States presents general information about Vietnamese history, culture, geography, government, and public services. This information gives a general overview of the country and offers a current view of Vietnam.

Radical Times: The Antiwar Movement of the 1960s (http:// library.thinkquest.org/27942). On this website, individuals can explore the antiwar movement that arose in the 1960s to oppose U.S. involvement in the Vietnam War. A timeline detailing the development of the movement, firsthand perspectives of those who participated in the protests, and general information about the counterculture, violence, and campus unrest, among other topics, can be found on the site.

The War in Vietnam: Escalation Phase (www.presidency. ucsb.edu/vietnam). Part of the American Presidency Project, this website offers information about the escalation of U.S. involvement in the war in Vietnam. It contains a list of short biographies of important players in the time leading up to and during the war, a timeline, and primary sources including newspaper articles from the period and official documents pertaining to the war.

INDEX